00⬛.678 B972
Bu⬛ rrows, Terry.- Blogs, wikis, Facebook, and

Br ⬤oklyn Branch
Ja⬤kson District Library   5/31/2012

Blogs, Wikis, Facebook, and More

WITHDRAWN

D0818381

Library of Congress Cataloging-in-Publication Data Is
available from the Library of Congress.

Cover illustration: Emily Brackett/Visible Logic

© 2012 by Terry Burrows

All rights reserved

First U. S. edition
Published by Chicago Review Press, Incorporated
814 North Franklin Street
Chicago, Illinois 60610

ISBN 978-1-61374-327-0

First published in Great Britain in 2011 by
Carlton Books Limited
20 Mortimer Street
London W1T 3JW

Editorial and design: The Orgone Company
Additional writing and research: Louis Burrows

Author's note: The internet is extremely fluid.
Websites, by their very nature, may come and go,
and will frequently alter in appearance. All of the
websites discussed and shown in this book are
correct as of October 2011.

Printed in China

5 4 3 2 1

Blogs, Wikis, Facebook, and More

2nd Edition

Everything You Want to Know About Using
Today's Internet but Are Afraid to Ask

Terry Burrows

CHICAGO
REVIEW
PRESS

Contents

Sites in bold are covered in greater detail.

004.678 B972
Burrows, Terry.- Blogs, wikis, Facebook, and

Brooklyn Branch
Jackson District Library

48   Communications

8x8; Aim; BigString; Blauk; BlueTie; BroadVoice; ContactOffice; DropBox; Dropsend; EBuddy; FastMail; FWD; Gadu-Gadu; **Gmail***; Google Talk; HamSphere; ICQ; InBox; Jabber; LavaBit; Lingo; LuxSci; Mediacom;* **Meebo***; MSN Hotmail; MXit; Myemail; MyWay; Ooma; Radvision; RingCentral;* **Skype***; Sendspace; SunRocket; Tempinbox; Trustmymail; Voicewing; Vonage; VZOchat; Xfire;* **YouSendIt***; Yahoo! Mail; Yahoo! Messenger.*

60   Design

Clickdensity; ColorBlender; Flickrlogomakr; Flower Maker; LogoSauce; Picreflect; Pixenate; Resizr; Typetester.

64   e-Commerce

AboutUs.org; Adgenta; **Amazon***; Ansearch;* **Auction Mapper***; Bigcartel; Billmonk; Blish; Cafépress; Castingwords; Carbonmade; Clipfire; Cooqy; Coverpop; Donorschoose;* **eBay***; Etsy; Flyspy; Fundable; Gumshoo; Hawkee; Oolsi;* **PayPal***; Qoop; Smarkets; Starting Point Directory; Stylehive; Wazima; Wists; Yelp; Yub; Zopa.*

70   Education and Knowledge

3Form; **7 Tips On***;* **Answers.com***; Askeet;* **Askville***;* **Answerbag***; Brainreactions; Bubbl.us; Copyscape; Echosign;* **eHow***; Gibeo; GuruLib; Hanzoweb; Helium;* **How Stuff Works***;* **HubPages***; Jots; Manage My Ideas;* **MetaGlossary***; Nuvvo; ProProfs; Quomon;* **Quotiki***; Root/vaults; Sparkhive;* **Squidoo***; Tractis; WisdomDB; Wondir;* **Yahoo! Answers***.*

112   Peer-to-Peer Sharing

*Anatomic P2P; BitComet; BitLord; BitSpirit;
BitTornado; **BitTorrent**; Demoniod; Fenopy; **isoHunt**;
LegalTorrents; MegaNova; Mininova; **SoulSeek**;
The Pirate Bay; Torrent; Torrentbox; Torrentmatrix;
Torrentportal; TorrentReactor; Torrents; TorrentScan;
TorrentSpy; uTorrent; Yotoshi; Vuze.*

120   Personal Management Tools

*1Time; **30 Boxes**; 88 Miles; Basecamp; Citadel;
ClockingIt; DekkoTime; Eventful; Harvest; **HipCal**;
Inventiondb; **MeetWithApproval**; Projectplace;
Remember the Milk; SlimTimer; **Ta-Da List**;
Taskfreak!; Taskspro; Time 59; Time IQ; TimeTracker;
ToadTime; Toggl; Trackslife; Trumba; Worktrec.*

128   Photographs and Videos

*23hq; Adultswim; Blip.TV; **Break**; Broadbandsports;
Clipshack; DailyMotion; Dropshots; **Flappr**; **Flickr**;
FlickrFling; Flyinside; Fotolia; Google Video; Groupr;
JumpCut; Mefeedia; **Metacafe**; Mightyv; Phlog;
Photobucket; Photomap; Revver; **Slide**; Slidestory;
Smilebox; **SmugMug**; **Stickam**; StupidVideos;
Tagworld; Truveo; Veoh; Videobomb; Videoegg;
Vidlife; **Vimeo**; **Webshots**; Yahoo! Video; **YouTube**;
ZippyVideos; Zoomer; Zoto.*

142   Podcasts

*@Podder; All Podcasts; AmigoFish; BlogMatrix Sparks!;
Digital Podcast; Doppler; EveryPodcast.com; fluctu8.
com; HappyFish; HardPodCafe; iPodderX; **iTunes**;*

142   Podcasts (Continued)

Juice; *Learn Out Loud; NetNewsWire; NewsFire; NewsMacPro; New Time Radio; Nutsie; Peapod; Phonecasting;* **PodBean***; Podcast Alley; Podcast Blaster; Podcast Central; Podcast Directory; Podcast Empire; PodcastPickle; Podcast Pup; Poddumfeeder; Podspider; Replay Radio; Revision3; RSSRadio; StreetIQ; Synclosure; TVTonic; WinAmp; Yamipod; Zencast.*

158   Portals

24eyes; Eskobo; Favoor; Feedtv; Googlemodules; **iGoogle***; Gritwire; Inbox; Itsastart; Klipfolio;* **Netvibes***; Pageflakes; Pobb; Protopage; Windowslive; Wrickr.*

164   Security Issues

12VPN; Avast! Pro; **Bitdefender***; Black Logic; ChicaPC-Shield; ESET NOD32; Express VPN; Happy VPN; Hide My Ass; Kaspersky; Lavasoft Ad-Aware; Liberty VPN; Malwarebytes; Norton Antivirus; Overplay;* **Pixelock***;* **Roboform***; Strong VPN; Super AntiSpyware; Swiss VPN; VyprVPN; Webroot Antivirus.*

170   Search Engines

Blekko*; Blogpulse; Exalead; Factbites; Gahooyoogle;* **Google***; Hakia; Healthline; Icerocket; Lexxe; Liveplasma; Makidi; Nextaris; Omgili; Prase us; Prefound; Quintura; Releton;* **Rollyo***; Surfwax;* **Swicki***; Technorati; Wikimatrix; Wink; Yoono;* **Yippy***; Yubnub.*

Introduction

It's been more than 15 years years since I first wrote professionally about technology, and the Internet in particular. The field has seen change during this period on an unprecedented scale. Since the middle of the 1990s, we have seen modes of social interaction, that a few decades earlier would have been in the realm of pure sci-fi fantasy, evolve swiftly into the everyday mundane. Barely four decades ago my parents were in awe of color television—technology that my generation has taken for granted. Similarly, while my eight-year-old son has been watching streamed children's TV shows on a laptop since the age of three—more recently designing his own websites and setting up his own blogs—I still marvel occasionally when I click on a link to a media-rich webpage that loads almost immediately, or when a colleague in New York e-mails an audio mp3 that he finished mixing a few minutes earlier and has taken barely a few seconds to reach me here in London. And the pace of change continues at a dazzling rate. I wrote the first edition of this book only four years ago, and yet would estimate that in excess of half of its original content has now had to be replaced.

Technostalgia
In its relatively short life, the Internet experience itself has changed beyond recognition. Even making a connection was once a task for the serious techhead. Now this process is all but transparent. Here's a personal illustration— and, to quote *Monty Python Live At Drury Lane*, "You try and tell the young people of today…they won't believe you!"

Let's go back to the Spring of 1995. At that time I was particularly fond of Radiohead's new album, *The Bends*. I'd read in a music paper that it was possible to "download" a video of the band's new single, "High and Dry," so decided to give it a go. I switched on my Apple Macintosh Quadra 650, and then an external 14.4 kilobyte modem—a black plastic box the size of a small paperback book with lots of flashing red lights. I first had to run a special program just to connect my computer to the Internet. After a few moments of high-pitched whirring and buzzing (a sound that now seems strangely nostalgic), a message flashed on screen telling me I was online. I then launched a web browser called *Mosaic* and typed in the URL. I clicked on a download button and then left it to do its thing. I returned to the computer about 30 minutes later to find that the Internet connection had failed. (It did this frequently.) I reconnected. Again—this time after about an hour—the connection failed. I decided to give it one final chance. After one hour the file still seemed to be transfering; another hour later, all was still good. Finally, after four-and-a-half hours, I was able to view a tiny, glitchy, low-resolution film. It was an underwhelming experience that also used up around 5 percent of my computer's tiny internal hard disk. Furthermore, not only was I paying around $30 a month to an ISP to have any sort of facility to connect to the Internet, I also had to pay the telephone company for about six hours worth of calls! And, of course, while I was hooked up to the Internet, my phone line was also tied up.

Fast-forward now to Summer 2011. I'm sprawled on a sofa with a MacBook Pro on my lap. I've just launched a web browser and typed in the URL for the world's most popular video site, *YouTube*. Seconds later I type into the search box: **"Radiohead High and Dry."** And I'm now watching that same video being streamed to me via a relatively modest 8-megabyte broadband line, connected via my home network Wi-Fi router. I pay an ISP roughly half the monthly fee I did 16 years ago, there's no additional charge for using the phone line, *and* I can make and receive calls while I'm connected. What's more, I could just as easily be doing this on my cellphone or watching it on a TV connected to the Internet through a games console. It's a pretty amazing development really.

Welcome to the Cloud

The fact that I can now watch videos on my laptop more easily and cheaply may not *seem* to be heralding a new way of life, but the implications are clear: If I can watch old music videos on demand, then why not entire TV shows or movies? Why do I need to buy DVDs? Why do we need TV channels? Or even a TV? If I can make video calls via my laptop, do I necessarily need a phone system? Indeed, these are all very real modern-day possibilities, even for those with modest technological capabilities.

So where will this all lead? One thing's for sure, information and other digital "content" will increasingly come to us via the Internet. CD and DVD may not *quite* be dead as formats, but more and more of us are choosing to download rather than buy hard copies—even if the sound and video quality is actually inferior. Unsurprisingly, as the web becomes increasingly central to our lives, businesses will increase their efforts in figuring out how to make us pay for the content they own. Already, major newspapers such as the *New York Times* and *Wall Street Journal* are only accessible to subscribers online via a "paywall." And peer-to-peer (P2P) or BitTorrent sites, where millions of users have frequently downloaded illegal digital content, find themselves under increasing legal pressure as multinational music and film corporations attempt to "educate" a generation of young users for whom music and film has always been "free."

In terms of the way we use the Internet, there is certain to be a continued gravitation toward web-based activity, or "cloud computing." (A buzzword guaranteed to sound as antequated in a few years time as "Web 2.0"—at the very center of the original edition of this book—does now!) In practice, In practise, the Cloud means simply that we can expect most of the software we previously bought and loaded onto our computers to be built into websites and accessed via a browser, and that instead of retaining banks of strorage drives our personal data is held by a third party and accessed via the web.

Of course, these are still the early days of an ongoing revolution, but there's already plenty of amazing stuff going on out there. And that's what this book is all about: helping you get the most out of your life online.

Changing Communications

So where did it all start? At the turn of the 1990s, a phenomenon emerged from the margins of the computer world with implications on the way we would operate and interact in the very near future—implications that few could have foreseen. It was around this period that computer scientists, technologists, and other geeky types began to appear in the mainstream media telling us how an "information superhighway" was about to knock the planet off its axis. In itself, the idea was relatively simple: all our personal computers would soon be connected in one enormous network, enabling us to communicate with each other and access enormous banks of data. Like all new technologies, "the Internet," as it was called, was difficult to use and didn't really work that well. Unsurprisingly, the early adopters were mostly other geeky types. Although this first wave of commercial Internet users may have talked about it with mind-numbing evangelical zeal, in practice it was largely used as an alternative to a telephone or a fax machine.

An Evolving World
Few of those early pioneering users could have imagined how different a place the world would be barely 20 years later. Now we find that social networking, e-mail, instant chat, and text messaging are far more common means of communication than any printed medium. After all, when was the last time you were sent a *handwritten* letter in the post? (And if you were, and it wasn't from an 80-year-old great aunt, wouldn't you think the sender was a bit . . . well . . . weird?) And what of the poor old fax machine? In the early 1990s, it was just beginning to migrate from the office to the home; by now most have been sent to their final resting place—the local dump.

If we look at what now represents modern Internet usage, we really do begin to see how our lives have been altered. We routinely order all manner of goods—books and DVDs, underpants and groceries—using online shops, often with "virtual" currencies like PayPal. We download our music, TV, and films, legally or otherwise, using peer-to-peer (P2P) software or digital music stores; we sell our unwanted stuff on eBay or other auction sites; we make our innermost thoughts available to the world via blogs and webpages; and we use Facebook and other social networking sites to communicate with and make friends.

Diverging Technologies
Let's also take a look at the changing face of hardware. Computing itself has become an increasingly mobile activity. More and more of us are moving away from cumbersome desktop systems, aided by a new generation of powerful wireless laptops. Most of us now have Wi-Fi systems in place in our homes, meaning that more and more of our computer activities have migrated from the desktop to the sofa. This revolution has also extended far beyond the boundaries of our homes: if you live in any reasonably sized town you're likely to find plenty of hot spots where you and your laptop can get access to the

The 2011 Apple iPad 2 tablet.

Internet. Indeed, go into any café in London, New York, or any other major city and you're sure to find a handful of surfers dotted around the room.

We can also now make phone calls from our laptops using software such as Skype, look at websites, perform our e-mail and social networking functions on our phones, and take photographs, videos, and audio recordings on both. Indeed, with the enormous popularity of the smartphone—driven initially by the massive worldwide success of Apple's iPhone—we have seen a single piece of technology bridge the gap between phone, computer, digital camera, and mp3 audio player. And in 2010, Apple—always at the cutting edge of design—breathed life into the touch-screen tablet market with its revolutionary iPad.

Internet access has further widened with popular game consoles, such as the Playstation 3, Wii, or XBox. Initially simply a means for gaming online, they are increasingly used as a means to view websites through the TV screen or as storage/playback for audio and video files.

Where Did It All Come From?

The Internet was actually an spin-off of one of the US government's late-'60s cold war initiatives—a stable, "packet switching" data communication system linking together military bases across the world that could withstand chunks of the system being taken out by some form of attack. On January 1, 1983, the US National Science Foundation took this network further, constructing a university backbone that would become the NSFNet. Many commentators view this date as the true birth of the Internet. Although only two years later this was opened up to commercial parties, it remained principally in the realm of academia for the rest of the decade.

The initial users were attracted by three distinct types of application: user groups and forums, where people with like-minded interests could exchange views or post questions; e-mail, which was basically an electronic postal system; and the World Wide Web, feted as the world's largest information retrieval system. The first two of these, of course, remain fundamental online practices, and, although the software may have evolved, the basic principles are pretty well unchanged. The Web, however, is a different matter altogether.

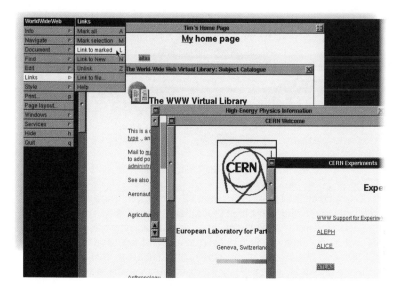

"Tim's Home Page" was the very first website.

Evolution of the Web

Jokingly referred to in the early days as the "World Wide Wait," the Web has evolved beyond all recognition. Early websites may well have been written in the same HTML code that most still are today, but connection and transmission speeds meant that the image-rich pages we now take for granted barely existed back then. After all, who would want to type in a URL only to wait 10 minutes for a page and its associated pictures to load?

So where exactly did the World Wide Web come from? It was the brainchild of British scientist Tim Berners-Lee. While working at CERN in Switzerland, the world's largest particle physics laboratory, he proposed a project based on the concept of a hypertext markup language (HTML) to enable researchers to share and update information. It was on August 6, 1991, that Berners-Lee put the first website live. Its URL was **http://info.cern.ch/hypertext/WWW/TheProject. html**, and it looked pretty much like a webpage in the modern sense. No screen grabs of this historic original page were ever taken, but an early example is shown above. Appropriately, "Tim's Home Page" provided an explanation of what the World Wide Web was. It was accessible on the world's first web browser known as *WorldWideWeb* and contained information on how to set up a web server. It was also the first web directory, since Berners-Lee maintained a list of other sites as they came into existence. From this historic birth, other innovators with more commercial and entrepreneurial vision gradually moved things in a different direction.

Technical Evolution

The "Web," as it soon became known, evolved at great speed. Browsers began to emerge with ever greater functionality and neat innovations, such as the ability to store (or "bookmark") websites, so that users didn't have to maintain a manual directory of web addresses if they wanted to revisit the site at a later date. However, it was with increased commercial connection speeds that the Web truly began to flourish. In 1995, the average Internet user went online via a 14.4 kilobytes-per-second modem link; nowadays, sixteen megabytes-per-second broadband connections are widely found in the home—that's over *1,000 times* faster. As these speeds increased, web designers have been able to enrich with images and sounds what had previously often been intentionally dull, text-based sites.

An Improved Web Experience

The earliest websites suffered from one major drawback: they were static objects, with no way for the users to interact with the page. Much of this was due to the fact that browser functionality was limited to simply interpreting HTML instructions to perform basic operations. Another reason was that Berners-Lee had only ever intended his invention to be a means for sharing information, not a means of entertainment. Nevertheless, as Internet usage broadened, it was clear that enhancing the Internet experience for the ordinary user was the way forward. The solutions took two forms: plug-ins and enhanced scripting. Both had the same goal in mind—boosting the power of the web browser.

Plug-in Software

Plug-ins were small add-on programs that were loaded into the browser to enable it to deal with specific types of media, such as animation or video. Many different plug-ins emerged, some of which were created with the sole aim of popularizing nonstandard or advanced file formats. The most widely accepted examples usually ended up integrated into new versions of the browser software; others quickly faded from view. Among the most significant plug-ins was Flash, which enabled movies and animations created using the Macromedia (now Adobe) Flash multimedia authoring system. In spite of Apple's refusal to enable Flash to be used on the IOS operating systems of its iPhone and iPad platforms, it remains one of the most commonly used methods of projecting such media on the Web, and Flash programming skills are a standard requirement among web designers.

Scripting Enhancements

Other important developments have come in the form of programming enhancements to the rather limited and basic HTML code used to create webpages. The most important of these was JavaScript. Developed in 1995 by Netscape, the company behind the Navigator web browser software—at that time the field leaders—JavaScript enabled web authors to design interactive sites with dynamic content. It was quickly integrated into the other major browsers (although Internet Explorer still only uses a subset of the language—JScript). Its importance is still being felt, as the now commonly used AJAX is itself a JavaScript-based technology.

The Internet Today

For the past four decades, progress in every area of computer technology has developed at a frantic rate. It already seems strange, for example, to think that the IT meltdown predicted at the turn of the 21st century was largely a result of space saving on databases designed during the middle of the 1980s. Because memory hardware was then at such a cost premium, one of the data analyst's tasks was to "normalize," avoiding duplicating data, and generally trying to use as little space as possible. One of the most widespread techniques was to store only the last two digits of the year, assuming that the "19" could be taken for granted. Safe in the knowledge that their designs would be obsolete within a few years, they were unconcerned that their systems might one day interpret the year "00" as 1900 rather than 2000, potentially throwing finance systems into chaos. Now, of course, most laptop computers can hold more data than an average 1980s mainframe, and storage that would once have cost tens of thousands of dollars can be bought for the price of a decent pair of sports shoes.

The Way We Work and Play

Technologists engage themselves in an endless drive to second-guess what the consumer doesn't yet know that he or she won't be able to live without. This has resulted in some bizarre and spectacular failures, as well as unpredictible successes—the widespread use of SMS messaging, along with the evolution of its own form of English language, could never have been imagined when it was developed as a means for businesspeople to organize meetings and communicate in brief without interrupting their work. And, quite clearly, Tim Berners-Lee's World Wide Web falls into the same category. Yet while the technology that underpins the Internet continues to evolve on a daily basis, the Web itself has been able to grow up in a more measured and "human" way.

In the middle of the first decade of the 21st century, a new buzzword began to gain circulation in the mainstream media. The term "Web 2.0" may have sounded like a milestone upgrade, or perhaps even a new version of the HTML code on which websites were built, but it was, in fact, nothing of the sort. Web 2.0 was altogether more of a philosophical idea, focusing on the growing importance of the Web, not only in the new and innovative ways in which designers were treating the platform, but in the changing behaviors of

The 2004 Web 2.0 Conference.

the end user.

The principles of Web 2.0 came about during a conference brainstorming session in 2003 organized by Internet media businessman Tim O'Reilly. It identified philosophical differences between an "old" Web ("Web 1.0") and the way in which it was evolving. The three most significant areas could be summarized as follows:

Dropbox, the "cloud" storage system.

1. **The Web as the central platform of Internet activity**
2. **The harnessing of collective knowledge**
3. **The creation of a "rich" user experience**

Of course, the term was quickly hijacked by both the marketing industry and the media, and by the end of the decade, Web 2.0 had long been rendered a meaningless term, usually associated with unconvincing corporate attempts at selling a new product as being somehow cutting edge. Yet while Web 2.0 may now have joined "Information Superhighway" in the lexicon of outmoded terminology, those three principles noted above are helpful in describing the trajectory in which online activity continues to evolve.

The Web as a Central Platform

"Cloud Computing" has become one of the more recent popular mainstream buzzwords. At its heart is the idea that standard computer functionality—software, data access, and storage, for example—is delivered via a web browser connected to the Internet and doesn't require the user to have any knowledge of the physical location or configuration of the system that delivers these functions. Thus, instead of needing to buy and install software on your computer for word processing, spreadsheets, presentations, or editing photographs and movies, it would simply be possible to perform all of these activities using applications *built into* the website itself and accessed through the web browser. The implications are similar for data storage, where it's now quite possible to rent remote storage space rather than maintaining banks of external hard drives and backups in the same location as your computer. And, of course, the same potential exists with digital entertainment—we don't necessarily have to download and store music, films, or TV shows, but we can simply watch or listen via a web browser. Almost all of the sites featured throughout this book fall into this category.

Harnessing Collective Knowledge

Diigo.com—ideal for tagging webpages.

Of all the ways in which the Internet has developed, it could be argued that those areas promoting social interaction have had the most impact on the world and the way in which we communicate with one another. Whether it be social networking through Facebook, creating a dialogue through blogs, tagging, and sharing websites using Del.icio.us or Diigo, or contributing collective knowledge on Wikipedia, some have argued that these developments herald a new dawn for democracy, personal creativity, and community. Others, however, believe that this will ultimately have a desocializing impact as we spend more and more of our time alone, shouting into a huge online abyss with nobody necessarily listening. It's clear, however, that while the fortunes of individual sites may fluctuate—the first edition of this book saw MySpace as the dominant force in social networking, with Facebook noted only as an emerging challenger—as generic concepts they have long passed through the novelty stage and, for many, are now as mundane as talking on the phone or sending text messages.

Of course, social networking and democracy are hardly new ideas as far as the Internet are concerned—indeed, they were central tenets of its foundation and evolution. Personal websites have been around since the beginning of the Web and have always been used as a means to express personal views. On the surface, blogging would not seem to be too far removed, except that the user can do it more easily and elegantly. However, there is this interactive aspect to consider: if we take two people speaking to one another as an analogy, the personal website is like delivering a lecture while the blog opens up the floor to questions and then possible dialogue.

One genuinely innovative area that seems to have evolved over the past decade is the way in which data can be combined from different sources. For example, it's possible to combine a photo gallery of bars tagged in Flickr with comments that people have written elsewhere about those bars and then connect the whole thing to Google Maps.

Rich User Experience

Many of us were so amazed by the World Wide Web in its early years of development that we were quick to forgive its shortcomings. It was slow, unreliable, and clunky to use. But it was worth the trouble. We're now in a new era where web designers have sought to recreate the interactivity of a computer desktop on the Web. This is often accomplished using new technologies such as AJAX. These new tools enable web applications to behave in ways that are familiar to us from our use of traditional desktop applications. For example, this could mean something as simple as integrating drag-and-drop techniques into a webpage. Such operations would once have been problematic, but the time delays caused by server calls are now mitigated by smaller amounts of information being sent asynchronously via JavaScript.

Of course, a major part of this user experience is the way in which we interact with the technology that provides our access to the Web. The standard QWERTY keyboard was adopted during the early days of personal computing primarily because it was assumed to be the next stage in the evolution of the traditional typewriter. Functionality was enhanced with the emergence of the mouse, which, although dating back to the 1950s, first appeared commercially with the Apple Lisa in 1983. Initially this new hardware met with some resistence, principally from those who were used to using both hands for typing, but has nonetheless remained the predominant means for on-screen navigation ever since.

These are not the only viable possibilities. Alternative interfaces have existed for some time; speech control software has been used by a small niche of users since the 1990s. However, the first competitor to the mouse/keyboard combination to gain widespread acceptance appeared in 2007. When Apple launched the first range of iPhones, the idea of touching the screen to control its functionality was alien to most users. Apple didn't conceive this idea—such designs were being discussed at the end of the 1960s—but was the first to introduce it successfully to a mass market. In 2010, the iPad tablet appeared—in essence, a much larger version of the iPhone, with the telephone

Apple Lisa, with the first commercial mouse.

function removed. In the space of less than two years, the iPad—and similarly designed counterparts—has become a serious competitor to the laptop for web-centered use in the home. These products invariably also feature a touch-screen keyboard to enable basic typing functions to be performed, but, away from web-based activities, software designers are finding increasingly interesting ways of exploiting this new tactile relationship—for example, editing photographic images by making specific movements on the screen.

Where Next?

Great fortunes can be made—and more commonly lost—trying to predict the Web's next big thing. And we certainly won't be adding our few cents here. We can be certain, though, of the ever-growing significance of cloud computing in the way our lives online are going to evolve—not to mention the impact these changes are sure to have on the way we live our lives away from the Web.

Blogging

A blog is an online diary or journal. The term is an abbreviation of "web log." Most blogs are recorded on a dedicated blogging website. They are user-generated, and entries are usually displayed in reverse chronological order. Blogs are widely used as diaries or to provide commentary or news on specific subjects. A typical blog combines text, images—sometimes sound and movies—and links to other related web pages. An important feature of blogging is that readers are able to leave their own personal comments. As of early 2011, there were 156 million active blogs in existence across the world.

Early Origins

The blog as we know it today evolved from the online web diary. Here, as the term suggests, people would keep a running account of their everyday personal lives. One particularly well-known example of an early news-based blog was the Drudge Report. Founded in 1994 by Matt Drudge, his website consists largely of links to

The Drudge Report, news from across the globe.

pro-conservative political news stories from the United States and international media. It is particularly noted for being the first news source to break the Bill Clinton/Monica Lewinsky scandal to the public. Matt Drudge himself is known to dislike having his famed site referred to as a blog, and it is now more properly recognized as a "news aggregation" site.

The first web logs were simple websites that were updated manually. Soon, however, tools began to appear that were able to facilitate the production and maintenance of articles posted in reverse chronological order. For the first time, this opened up the blogging process to a larger group of users—those lacking the technical skills (or desire) to create html webpages. Ultimately, this resulted in the creation of the browser-based software, such as Wordpress or Blogger, that now predominates.

Engadget, a popular technology blog.

When Blogs Go Bad!

Given the popularity and personal nature of many blogs, it's not surprising that some have ended up with unexpected consequences for the bloggers themselves. Areas of legal concern have included the release of confidential information or making defamatory remarks. There are also an increasing number of well-documented cases of employees losing their jobs for publishing details of their working or personal lives. In fact, this is now sufficiently commonplace to have evolved its own specific term: to be "dooced" is to be fired from your job for something you've written on the Internet. This comes from the case of Heather Armstrong in Salt Lake City, Utah, who, in 2002, was fired from her job as a web designer for writing a satirical blog about her experiences at a dot-com startup company—she wrote under the pseudonym of "Dooce." She later offered would-be bloggers some sound advice: "I was fired from my job because I had written stories that included people in my workplace. My advice to you is BE YE NOT SO STUPID."

• In 2005, US blogger Aaron Wall was sued by Traffic Power for defamation and publication of trade secrets. He exposed what he alleged were attempts to rig search engine results on Google. The case was keenly observed by bloggers because it addressed the legal issue of who is liable for comments posted on a blog.

• In 2006, Ellen Simonetti, a flight attendant with Delta Airlines, was fired for comments made on her blog, "Queen of the Sky," which also showed her posing in her work uniform. The company argued that a blogger's activities could be capable of adversely affecting an employer's brand.

• The same year, Jessica Cutler—"The Washingtonienne"—blogged about her sex life while being employed as a congressional assistant. She was dismissed after the blog was discovered but later went on to write a novel based on her experiences, earning a reported $300,000 publishing advance.

• In 2007, Egyptian blogger Kareem Amer was sentenced to a four-year prison term, having been charged with insulting President Mubarak and Islam as well as inciting sedition through his blog.

• In Britain, college lecturer Tracy Williams anonymously contributed to a blog in which she referred to political candidate Michael Keith-Smith as a Nazi. Her identity was easily traced by her ISP, and in 2006 she was successfully sued for £10,000 ($20,000) in damages and £7,200 ($14,000) in costs.

• In 2010, Bilal Zaheer Ahmad, a 23-year-old British blogger, was arrested on terrorism charges after he posted comments on an Islamic fundamentalist blog encouraging the murder of British MPs who had voted in favor of the war in Iraq. In spite of the claims in court that his post was intended to be "tongue-in-cheek...an ironic gesture," the young IT graduate found himself with a 12-year prison sentence.

Evolution of Blogging

As is often the case in any field of endeavor, there is no clear agreement as to who invented blogging. Certainly one widely quoted candidate is Justin Hall, who, in January 1994, while a student at Swarthmore College in Pennsylvania, created Justin's Links from the Underground. Starting as an early guide to the Internet, it gradually evolved to incorporate intimate details of

Justin's Home Page

Welcome to my first attempt at Hypertext

Howdy, this is twenty-first century computing... (Is it worth our patience?) I'm publishing t

High Stylin' **on the Wurld Wyde Webb**

This is a Hypertext server using MacHTTP v1.2.3 running on a Powerbook 180 w/ 8 RAM here at Swarthmore College in Swarthmore, Pennsylvania.

I put this together with MacHTTP and the assistance of NCSA's HTML Primer that was in waste vastland. More general information about HyperText Mark-up Language is also ava here.

Justin's Home Page, arguably the first blog.

Hall's own everyday life. In December 2004, *New York Times Magazine* referred to him as "the founding father of personal blogging." However, it was several years before blogging started to take off in a big way. To give an illustration as to how things developed, within a year of its launch in 1996, the website Xanga had only 100 online diaries; by the start of 2006 there were well over 20 million.

The popularity of blogging rocketed when the first hosted blog tools began to appear in the late 1990s, with OpenDiary being credited as the first blog community where readers could add comments to blog entries written by others. In August 1999, Pyra Labs launched Blogger, a free service that provided an easy set of tools that any person could use to easily set up a blog.

The first blogs to make a big impression were political in nature, with names such as Andrew Sullivan, Ron Gunzburger, and Taegan Goddard coming to prominence. Indeed, in 2002, blogging was largely responsible for forcing the resignation of US Senator Trent Lott from a leadership post, when a speech honoring former presidential candidate Strom Thurmond was interpreted by some as supporting racial segregation. The mainstream media only started reporting the story after it had arisen from the blogging community. This gave a boost in credibility to the idea of blogging as a serious medium of news dissemination.

Blogging evolved further during the war in Iraq, with Iraqi bloggers such as Salam Pax gaining widespread readership in the West. Additionally, many "warblogs" were created by serving military personnel, giving readers new perspectives on the realities of war, as well as alternative viewpoints from official news sources.

Blogging is now more popular than ever. A recent study estimates that

Etymology

The term "web log" was first used in 1997, coined by Jorn Barger in his influential early blog Robot Wisdom. He used it to describe the process of, as he put it, "logging the web" while he surfed. The shorter form was introduced two years later by Peter Merholz, who jokingly cut the world "weblog" into the phrase "we blog" on his website. This was quickly adopted as both a noun and a verb.

over 40 million Americans are now regular readers. This in itself may present certain problems, as increasing numbers of consumers receive their news from sources that may lack the credibility of that provided by a bona fide professional journalist. President Barack Obama has himself expressed concern at the growing influence of blogging on society: "If the direction of the news is all blogosphere, all opinions, with no serious fact-checking, no serious attempts to put stories in context, that what you will end up getting is people shouting at each other across the void but not a lot of mutual understanding."

How to Start Blogging

A blog can, if you so choose, be a deeply personal document. You could think of it as being a cross between a personal telephone call and a newspaper column. You can share your favorite recipes, make public your most intimate thoughts, or, if so inclined, go off on the wildest of political rants. Also increasingly popular, are corporate or organizational blogs. If your work catches on throughout the blogosphere there is also the additional potential for earning advertising revenue.

Curiously, given that blogging and its associated software evolved out of the growth of personal websites, recent years have seen a growing use of blogging sites/software such as WordPress as a *replacement for* the traditional website. This can be attributed in part to the ease of use of the best web-based software—elegant and professional-looking pages can be created in a matter of minutes without the need of any specialized software skills. And, in most cases, setting up a blog is absolutely free.

Of course, with millions of blogs now fighting for attention, yours will have to be something special to gain any great public attention, so before you begin it's worth putting some serious planning and thought into what you are about to do. Here are a few basic steps to getting on the blogging ladder.

Decide on your theme There are two distinct approaches to blogging: write on whatever subject happens to interest you at any moment in time—rather like entries in a diary—or select a single theme and stick with it. Unless you're already well known, if you want your blog to develop a following, the latter approach will be better—people with similar interests are more likely to keep returning for more. Of course, if your blog is intended to represent a company or official body, then there will naturally be a different agenda here.

Choose your service Choose from an online web-based approach or downloadable software. There are many developer-hosted blog sites from which you can choose, among them Xanga (**www.xanga.com**), Blogger (**www.blogger.com**), LiveJournal (**www.livejournal.com**), and Serendipity (**www.s9y.org**). The downloadable alternative is, in essence a word processor for blogging—you can write when you're not online and then upload your post when you connect to the Internet. Examples include b2evolution (**http://b2evolution.net**) and Ecto (**http://illuminex.com/ecto**). WordPress (**www.wordpress.com**) is available in both options.

Customize your space Most blog spaces give you a high degree of control over the way they look. You can decide on the colors, number of columns, and the overall look of your page, or use/modify preset themes. You may also want to consider adding media, such as images, sounds, or video clips.

Get writing This is the difficult part. The best advice for novice writers is to keep posts brief and write about what you know. If you have specialist information, your blog is more likely to gain a following. Many bloggers begin with an introductory post, telling prospective readers why they have started their blog and the kinds of things they intend to write about. Be confident: if you're taking the trouble to create a blog, it's presumably because you want others to read your work.

Develop your persona Before you finalize your blog, take a look at as many others as possible. See what your rivals are doing, and note the things you like and dislike. You'll see quickly that there is more to most blogs than just the posts themselves. Many blogging applications allow you to add your own lists to your page. Here you can note the books you are reading or music you are listening to. You can also incorporate third-party services into your blog, enabling your readers to subscribe to your site.

Going public You must have a means of notifying tracking sites that your blog exists and updates are being made, otherwise you will never find or maintain an audience. So before you choose your blogging service, you need to establish if it automatically "pings" the most important weblog tracking sites. This means checking if your service (or offline software) sends notifications to specific blog tracking sites to alert them that you have set up your blog or posted a new entry. This, in turn, will open your blog out to the most important search engines. Most of the modern blogging systems—web-based or otherwise—will do this for you automatically, as well as offering other alternatives like an RSS feed, effectively enabling users to subscribe to your blog, or click-on links to social networking sites such as Facebook or Twitter. (You may even be able to "send" certain blog entries as "Tweets" or Facebook status updates.) If your blogging service does not perform automatic notifications, you will need to use third party software, such as Pingomatic (**http://pingomatic.com**) or Bl.ogs (**http://blo.gs/ping.php**). These will allow you to choose which tracking sites you wish to update.

Pingomatic, notifies blog tracking sites.

Build a relationship with your readers There's only one way to gain a following and that's by making frequent postings—you can think of that as Blogging 101! If people like what you write, they will come back; if there's nothing new to read, they will quickly lose interest. At some point, it comes down to making a commitment and sticking to it. And don't forget, the more you blog, the better you'll become at it.

Blogger

http://www.blogger.com

Launched by Pyra Labs in 1999, Blogger was one of the earliest dedicated blog-publishing tools, and it is widely believed to have helped popularize the format. In February 2003, Pyra Labs was bought out by Google. Blogs can now either be hosted on Google's server (on the **blogspot.com** domain), externally on a user's own domain, or on the user's own server.

Creating Your First Blog

Now let's take a look at how to use Blogger and create a space of your own.

• Enter **www.blogger.com** in your web browser. (Since Blogger is now a part of the Google empire, you first need to enter Google account details on the right of the screen. If you don't have an account, click on **Get Started**, and follow the instructions until you are logged in.)

• In the home page, click on the arrowed button marked **Create A Blog**. On the resulting screen, create a title for your blog and then create a unique URL where it will reside. When you've chosen a name, enter it in the **Blog Address (URL)** box and click on **Check Availability**. This will tell you if that name has already been taken. Now click on the **Continue** arrow.

• Blogger provides you with a number of preset visual templates. Choose one and then click on the **Continue** arrow. (Don't worry for now about which template you choose—it can easily be changed later.)

• The screen that next appears will confirm that your blog has been set up and is ready for action. To write your first blog entry, click on the arrow marked **Start Blogging**.

• Now all you have to do is write your blog. Rather than composing text online, many bloggers prefer to write using conventional word processing software and then copy-and-paste into the text box on Blogger. Before you decide to publish, you can click on the **Preview** button to see how it will look. If you don't get the opportunity to finish, you can click on **Saved** and go back to it another time. When you're happy with your work, click on the **Publish Post** button.

• You'll now see a window confirming that your blog has been published. You can now either view your post, edit your post or create a new one. Click on **View Post** to see how your entry will appear to the world.

• If you want to change anything about your blog or an individual post, click on **Design** at the top right-hand corner of the screen. (Note: you must still be logged into your Blogger account to do so.) This takes you to the Dashboard window where you will find overview information about all of your blogs. It is here you can alter the settings for your different blogs.

• The Dashboard lists each of the blogs you have created for that specific Blogger account. Beneath each entry you have options for creating new posts or editing existing posts and comments. If you click on **Settings**, this provides you with a variety of options for redesigning the appearance of your blog; here you can either edit elements of the existing template or choose a different template altogether.

Other Blogging Sites

The list shown below concentrates on those sites that are primarily aimed at writing or editing blogs. They are all what is termed "developer-hosted" sites, meaning that they are web-based applications.

BattleBlog	www.battleblog.com	LiveJournal	www.livejournal.com
Bitty	www.bitty.com	Posterous	www.posterous.com
Blip	www.blip.tv	Qumana	www.qumana.com
Blog.com	www.blog.com	Serendipity	www.s9y.org
Blogger	www.blogger.com	Squarespace	www.squarespace.com
Blogs	http://blo.gs	Talkr	www.talkr.com
Blurb	www.blurb.com	Tumblr	www.tumblr.com
Cocomment	www.cocomment.com	WordPress	www.wordpress.com
Feedblitz	www.feedblitz.com	Xanga	www.xanga.com
LifeType	www.lifetype.com		

Offline Blogging Software

Here is a list of some of the most useful offline blogging software. They all have their own websites where they can be downloaded free of charge.

Apache Roller	http://rollerweblogger.org	LiveJournal	http://www.livejournal.com
B2evolution	http://b2evolution.net	Mephisto	http://mephistoblog.com
BBlog	http://www.bblog.com	Nucleus	http://www.nucleuscsm.com
Blosxom	http://www.blosxom.com	Pivotlog	http://www.pivotlog.net
DotClear	http://www.dotclear.net	Serendipity	http://www.s9y.org
Drupal	http://www.drupal.org	Slash	http://www.slashcode.com
Ecto	http://illuminex.com/ecto	Subtext	http://subtextproject.com
Geeklog	http://www.geeklog.net	Textpattern	http://textpattern.com
LifeType	http://www.lifetype.net	WordPress	http://www.wordpress.com

Bookmarks and Tagging

Just as we are able to place markers in a real book to remind of us of the page we've reached, or as a pointer to a piece of information we want to revisit in the future, we can do the same on the Internet. Of course, this is not a new idea: almost every browser developed since the birth of the web has had some kind of facility for storing and organizing URLs (the addresses) of favorite websites, allowing the user to return there at the click of a button. More recently, however, web-based applications have emerged, creating more sophisticated approaches to bookmarking or "tagging."

Multiple Tags

So what are these new developments? And do they really offer anything fundamentally different from the features included within our good old traditional web browsers? A fundamental development is in that data storage—as with many of the applications being discussing in this book—is migrated from the desktop to the web, so when you bookmark a URL, it's no longer retained by your browser but stored on an external web server. The principal advantages are that you can access your collection of bookmarks on any computer, anywhere in the world, irrespective of browser type or even computer platform. Furthermore, there's the safety dimension: if some disaster befalls your computer, and your data is not backed up, then your bookmarks will be lost; if you're using web-based bookmarks, this can never happen.

More significantly, perhaps, these new-style applications recognize that the most useful information retrieval systems require any piece of information to be stored under a *variety* of different categories. Traditional browser-based systems such as Safari (*shown below*) enable bookmarks to be stored *only* within a single suitably named folder—perhaps **news**, **sports**, **music**, or **cinema**. To retrieve a page the user would have to know exactly which category folder it had been stored in, or else flick through every single bookmark that had been saved. Dedicated bookmarking applications, however, allow for the

Traditional bookmarking on the Safari browser.

allocation of any number of category "tags" to any stored bookmark. So, for example, a story from the *New York Times* about the political situation in Libya might be tagged under a number of different categories: **New York Times**, **Libya**, **Africa**, **Qaddafi**, **Libyan Rebels**, **NATO**, or any other tag the user might deem suitable. It then becomes possible to view all of the bookmarks associated with any tag as a single list.

Social Bookmarking

Applying multiple tags would clearly enable us to organize our bookmarks in a much more sophisticated way than was hitherto possible using traditional browser bookmarking features. However, perhaps the most radical aspect of this development is what has been termed "social bookmarking." This means that if you use one of these bookmarking websites, you may also make your stored information available to the rest of the world. This enables ranked lists of universal bookmarks to be created within any category. Furthermore, some websites—such as Del.icio.us—even create the possibility of communication with other users who have similar bookmarks.

It could be argued, in fact, that sharing tagged information in this way is a more effective technique for locating useful data on the Internet than by typing entries into traditional search engines such as Yahoo! or Google. This is based on the premise that all tag-based classification is done by real people, who understand the content of the webpage, rather than search engine software "spiders" that algorithmically attempt to figure out whether a piece of data is likely to be relevant.

Of course, as we've already discussed in relation to other socially-oriented Internet activities, the more people who use the application, the "richer" it becomes—as greater numbers of people bookmark the pages they find useful, the higher the page ranking. Thus, if you take a look at any single category, the entries at top end of the list will be the pages bookmarked by the most people.

Folksonomy

The idea of the entire population of end users creating and naming categories according to their own free will is known—somewhat disparagingly in some circles—as a "folksonomy." And this presents simultaneously the greatest strength and the greatest weakness of the whole notion of social bookmarking. A professionally created taxonomy—a term describing any system of categorization—will usually have been developed by informed sources and will use unambiguous terminology and will generally comprise a sophisticated hierarchy. A folksonomy, on the other hand, is open ended. It can be created quickly, on the fly, and molded entirely to the needs of any individual. Thus, critics of using a folksonomy as a basis for indexing and retrieving information would argue that the overall effectiveness of the system is heavily defused by polysemy (tags having multiple related meanings), synonyms (tags with the same or similar meanings), or simple inflections or misspellings. These are largely academic arguments, however, that fail to take into account quite simply how useful it can be to create a categorization system geared entirely to one's own requirements.

Delicious

http://www.delicious.com

The first social bookmarking website we'll take a look at is Delicious. Founded in 2003 by Joshua Schachter, Delicious was siginificantly responsible for the popularity of the whole tagging concept.

Like many modern Internet entrepreneurs, Joshua Schacter is a self-confessed "geeky guy," who created and ran Delicious largely on his own while still holding down a day job as a programmer for Morgan Stanley in New York City. He turned full time on his project in March 2005, but by the end of that year had sold Delicious to Yahoo! for a figure rumored to be in the region of $30 million. Interestingly, the website's name was originally styled **Del.icio.us**, and featured the unusual URL of **http://del.icio.us**. Although this may seem a little odd, lacking the usual "www" prefix, this is an example of what is known as a "domain hack"—an unconventional domain name created by combining domain labels to spell out a "real" name. The conventional spelling was adopted after the site's 2008 redesign.

At the end of 2010, to the horror of many the website's core users, Yahoo! declared that Delicious was to be "sunsetted"—which many interpreted as being shut down permanently. Happily, in April 2011, Avos Systems bought the site, taking over its running four months later. Delicious now claims around 6 million users worldwide, with over 200 million unique bookmarked URLs.

The Delicious concept is extremely simple: a non-hierarchical keyword indexing system where users can tag their bookmarks with any number of freely chosen category names. Everything posted to Delicious is publicly viewable by default, although users are able to mark specific bookmarks as private if they so wish. A combined universal view of all bookmarks with a given tag is available—for instance, the URL **http://www.delicious.com/tag/sports** will display all of the most recent links that have been tagged **sports**. A new feature since the Avos buy-out are "stacks"—or what Delicious refers to as "playlists for the web." This takes on board some of the scrapbook features offered by other sites, and offers and easier way of storing, reading and sharing your collections.

As its default setting, the Delicious homepage features tabs labeled **Featured Stacks** and **Featured Links**, which shows some of the most popular collections of tags and stacks.

How Does Delicious Work?

As a website, Delicious is very simple to use. Once you've created your own account, with a user ID and password, you are asked to drag a button labeled **Save on Delicious** to the toolbar of your web browser. Clicking this button while you are browsing will give you the option of bookmarking the website you are currently viewing, adding tags or adding it to one of your own existing stacks. (Note: for those of you who are nervous about the idea of storing personal data on a remote server, Delicious bookmarks can also be exported into most of the popular Internet browsers, so personal back-ups can be made.)

So let's take a more detailed look at some of the features you can expect to use in Delicious, beginning with the account creation process.

Registration

Let's begin by creating a Delicious account and setting up the posting button in your browser.

• Enter the URL **http://www.delicious.com** in your web browser. You'll be directed to the Delicious home page. To get started, click on the **Join** button.

• This takes you to the registration page. Enter your chosen **delicious ID**—the name you want to be identified to other Delicious users. (The system will check if this ID is already taken.) Also add a **password**, and **e-mail address**. Delicious also requires you to enter the security "captcha." Finally, click on the **Join** button.

The welcome screen tells you how to install your Delicious **Save links** button.

• Click on the text labeled **Save on Delicious** and then drag and release it into the menu bar of your web browser.

The first social bookmarking website we'll take a look at is Delicious. Founded in 2003 by Joshua Schachter, Delicious was siginificantly responsible for the popularity of the whole tagging concept.

Like many modern Internet entrepreneurs, Joshua Schacter is a self-confessed "geeky guy," who created and ran Delicious largely on his own while still holding down a day job as a programmer for Morgan Stanley in New York City. He turned full time on his project in March 2005, but by the

end of that year had sold Delicious to Yahoo! for a figure rumored to be in the region of $30 million. Interestingly, the website's name was originally styled **Del.icio.us**, and featured the unusual URL of **http://del.icio.us**. Although this may seem a little odd, lacking the usual "www" prefix, this is an example of what is known as a "domain hack"—an unconventional domain name created by combining domain labels to spell out a "real" name. The conventional spelling was adopted after the site's 2008 redesign.

At the end of 2010, to the horror of many the website's core users, Yahoo! declared that Delicious was to be "sunsetted"—which many interpreted as being shut down permanently.

Happily, in April 2011, Avos Systems bought the site, taking over its running four months later. Delicious now claims

around 6 million users worldwide, with over 200 million unique bookmarked URLs.

The Delicious concept is extremely simple: a non-hierarchical keyword indexing system where users can tag their bookmarks with any number of freely chosen category names. Everything posted to Delicious is publicly viewable by default, although users are able to mark specific bookmarks as private if they so wish. A combined universal view of all bookmarks with a given tag is available—for instance, the URL **http://www.delicious.com/tag/sports** will display all of the most recent links that have been tagged **sports**. A new feature since the Avos buy-out are "stacks"—or what Delicious refers to as "playlists for the web." This takes on board some of the scrapbook features offered by other sites, and offers and easier way of storing, reading and sharing your collections.

As its default setting, the Delicious homepage features tabs labeled **Featured Stacks** and **Featured Links**, which shows some of the most popular collections of tags and stacks.

How Does Delicious Work?

As a website, Delicious is very simple to use. Once you've created your own account, with a user ID and password, you are asked to drag a button labeled **Save on Delicious** to the toolbar of your web browser. Clicking this button while you are browsing will give you the option of bookmarking the website you are currently viewing, adding tags or adding it to one of your own existing stacks. (Note: for those of you who are nervous about the idea of storing personal data, Delicious bookmarks can also be exported into most of the popular internet browsers, so personal back-ups can be made.)

So let's take a more detailed look at some of the features you can expect to use in Delicious, beginning with the account creation process.

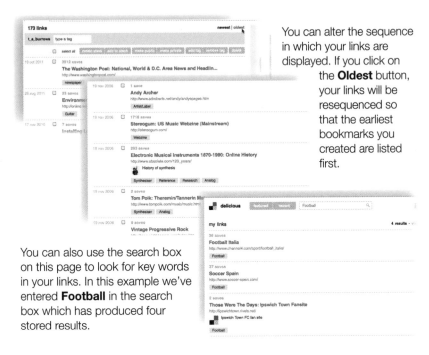

You can alter the sequence in which your links are displayed. If you click on the **Oldest** button, your links will be resequenced so that the earliest bookmarks you created are listed first.

You can also use the search box on this page to look for key words in your links. In this example we've entered **Football** in the search box which has produced four stored results.

Creating A New Bookmark

Once you've set up the menu-bar button, bookmarking and viewing pages is a very simple process. Here we'll bookmark the *Washington Post's* website.

• Opening your browser and type in the URL for the *Washington Post*—that's **http:///www. washingtonpost.com**.

• To store this website, you simply click on the button labeled **Save on Delicious** in your browser's menu bar. (Note: You must, of course, already be logged into Delicious to be able to do this.)

• This will open up the **Add Link Details** window, enabling you to store information about your bookmark: The name, the URL, the tags you've set up, and 1,000 letters of descriptive text. For now we'll set a single tag called **newspaper**—which you can do simply by typing the text into the box marked

Add Tags. (Alternatively, Delicious offers you some recommended tapgs that ve already been used with this site: you can add any of these tags simply by clicking on them.)

• If you want to make this link a private one, tick the box on the bottom left of the window. When you are finished, click on the **Save** button to store your bookmark.

Tagging with Delicious

It would, of course, be quite possible to view your bookmarks as a single list, scrolling through until you find exactly what you're looking for. That's fine if you only have a few bookmarks stored, but a dull, time-consuming process if you have several thousand. So Delicious makes life easier by enabling you to apply tags to any bookmark you've saved. A tag is simply a category that enables you to store bookmarks into meaningful groups of your own choosing. In the bookmark set up for the *Washington Post*, you already applied a tag—**Newspaper**. If you now to look at your list of tags (which can be found on the right of your Delicious screen) and click on **Newspapers**, ONLY bookmarks for those sites that have been similarly tagged will appear on the screen.

Multiple Tags

So is this approach *really* so different from keeping bookmarks in categorized folders within your web browser? Absolutely. The power of Delicious—and other similar sites—is that it allows you to apply *more than one* tag to any link.

Let's look at the entry you created for the *Washington Post*. Click on the **Edit** button alongside the link.

This reopens up the **Add Link Details** window. The box labeled **Add Tags** already contains an entry for **Newspaper**. We might also type in other relevant tags, such as **Washington**, **Politics**, and **News**. To do this, simply type in the text and press the **comma** key to create the tag. When you have finished, click on the **Save Changes** button.

If you now look at the *Washington Post* bookmark in the list you will see that the three new tags have been added. Each of these tags is a button that can be clicked on to select other grouped bookmarks—if you were now to click on **Washington**, only bookmarks that you had similarly tagged would be listed.

Uses For Multiple Tags

Clearly, then, Delicious enables users to create a very powerful indexing and cross-referencing system that no standard web browser could match—indeed, it offers levels of versatility only previously possible on database software. To give a practical example, if you were to bookmark a series of websites containing cocktail recipes, you might create tags for their ingredients so that if, say, you clicked on a tag marked "rum," you could expect to get a list of all the cocktails you have bookmarked that featured rum as one of its ingredients.

If you are currently maintaining an ever-expanding, complex set of bookmarks within your browser, you should seriously consider a web-based solution like Delicious. Even just as means for organization information it's truly capable of radically enhancing your online experience.

Creating Stacks

A recent feature of post-Yahoo! Delicious, stacks are an alternative way of displaying groups of bookmarks. Rather than using folksonomy tags, the user simply groups them under a heading of their choice. Let's take a look at creating a stack. Click on your Delicious ID and select **My Stacks** from the drop-down menu.

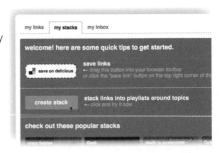

• The **Create A Stack** window opens. Enter a name for your stack and a description of the links you plan to include. To include bookmarks that you've already stored click on the **Add Saved Links** button.

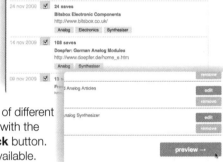

• Work through your list of links, checking the selection box for each one you want to include. An effective shortcut maybe to choose a related tag and tick the **Select All** button. At the foot of the list click on the **Preview** button.

• You can now see how your stack will appear. You can select a variety of different types of view. When you are happy with the contents, click on the **Publish Stack** button. This will make your stack publicly available.

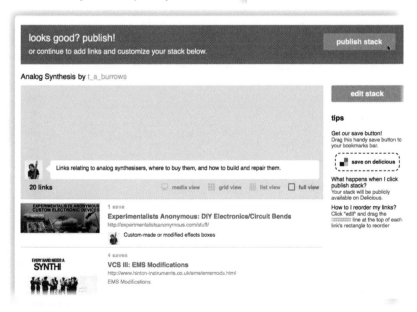

looks good? publish!
or continue to add links and customize your stack below.

publish stack

Analog Synthesis by t_a_burrows

edit stack

tips

Get our save button!
Drag this handy save button to your bookmarks bar.

save on delicious

What happens when I click publish stack?
Your stack will be publicly available on Delicious.

How to I reorder my links?
Click "edit" and drag the line at the top of each link's rectangle to reorder

Links relating to analog synthesisers, where to buy them, and how to build and repair them.

20 links media view grid view list view full view

EXPERIMENTALISTS ANONYMOUS CUSTOM ELECTRONIC DEVICES

1 save
Experimentalists Anonymous: DIY Electronics/Circuit Bends
http://experimentalistsanonymous.com/stuff/
Custom-made or modified effects boxes

EVERY BAND NEEDS A
SYNTHI

4 saves
VCS III: EMS Modifications
http://www.hinton-instruments.co.uk/ems/emsmods.html
EMS Modifications

Digg

http://www.digg.com

Digg is a news website that combines social bookmarking and blogging with democratic editorial control. Stories are chosen for the site not by an editor but by community members.

News stories and websites are submitted by Digg users, and appear in an **Upcoming Stories** list on the main page. These can then be ranked by other users by clicking a "digg it" symbol. Entries with the highest number of "diggs" will appear in the **Popular Stories** list. Each one may be tagged and searched under a number of different categories. All stories fall under one of the main headings of **Technology**, **Science**, **World & Business**, **Sports**, **Entertainment**, and **Gaming**. There is a separate area in which videos and podcasts can also be "dugg."

On the surface, Digg would appear to be democratic in its aim of highlighting the most popular stories on the Internet. However, critics have claimed that self-censorship enables sensationalism or misinformation to thrive. Furthermore, Digg also has a facility to "bury" stories—if a sufficient number of "buries" are received, the story is dropped from the website. This feature is intended to allow users to filter out spam, but there's some suspicion that it may have been used by groups of people to remove stories containing opinions countering their own.

Digg was created by Californian Internet celebrity Kevin Rose and launched at the end of 2004. In 2009 it launched its Facebook Connect feature, enabling Facebook users to integrate Digg postings with their updates. Digg is now ranked among the 150 most heavily used websites online—as of 2011, Quantcast estimates that the site receives more than 7 million unique visits per month.

Digg in Action

To try out Digg for yourself, type **http://www.digg.com** into your web browser. When the main screen appears, click on the tab marked **Most Recent** and then from the drop-down menu **7 Days**. What follows is a list of the stories to have been submitted over the past week with the most "diggs." Other options exist for similarly popular stories over the last day, month, and year.

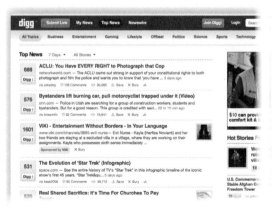

To view a story from the list, all you have to do is click on the title, which opens the URL in a new browser window. To "digg" a story, click the **Digg it** button to the left of the URL.

Submitting an Article

Begin by finding a story you wish to add to Digg and making a note of its URL. Before you submit an article, you must first be registered and logged in: if you are registered, click on the **Login** button; if you are new to Digg click on the **Join Digg!** button and follow the registration instructions.

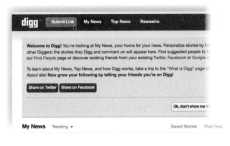

• To make a submission, begin by clicking on the tab at the top of the screen marked **Submit Link**.

• Enter the link in the pop-up window. You needn't worry about the "http://" part of the URL. Click on **Submit**.

• Give your story a title and a description. Select a category from the drop-down menu. To submit your story click on the **Digg It!** button.

• You are now taken to the comments window for your article. This tells you that the story has now been set up on Digg and other registered users can begin adding information. A summary of users responses is shown at the foot of the page.

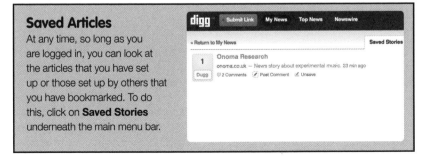

Saved Articles

At any time, so long as you are logged in, you can look at the articles that you have set up or those set up by others that you have bookmarked. To do this, click on **Saved Stories** underneath the main menu bar.

StumbleUpon

http://www.stumbleupon.com

Another approach to bookmarking websites is the recommendation system used by StumbleUpon, which is sometimes referred to as a "discovery engine." StumbleUpon works by using the toolbar installed at the top of the screen, which enables its users to discover and rate webpages, photos, videos, and news articles and recommend them to other like-minded users. When you join StumbleUpon, you tick a list of category interests. Relevant webpages appear when the user clicks the **Stumble** button on the browser's toolbar— StumbleUpon decides which new webpage to display based on the user's ratings of previous pages, ratings by friends, and the ratings of users with similar interests. The new webpage can be rated using the **thumbs up** or **thumbs down** buttons.

StumbleUpon uses what is known as "collaborative filtering," a combination of human opinion and automated interpretation of a user's personal preference, to create a social network. Users thus "stumble upon" pages explicitly recommended by friends, peers, and like-minded people.

StumbleUpon was launched in November 2001 by a group of Canadian post-graduate students and sold to eBay in 2007 for $75 million. Two years later, Garrett Camp and Geoff Smith—two of the and original founders—bought the company back. It now has over 15 million registered users.

Using StumbleUpon

Enter **http://www.stumbleupon.com** in your web browser and on the homepage click on the button marked **Join For Free**. Once you've worked through the registration process, you will be taken to the **Category** screen, where you must click on at least five areas of interest. These will influence your suggested websites. When you you finished your selection, click on the button marked **Save Interests**.

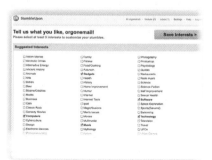

This next page you see will give you an overview of the StumbleUpon toolbar, which appears at the top of the screen. The key component here is the **Stumble** button, on the far left of the toobar. Each time you click on this button, a "recommended" web will open. You can read the page and rate it one way or another using the **thumbs up** or **thumbs up** buttons. The **Share** button enables you to send recommendations to friends or other "Stumblers." Sharing can also be done using the major social networking sites, Facebook and Twitter. The rest of the toolbar enables you to bookmark your chosen websites.

On the surface, this may seem like a slightly random form of web surfing. And yet, as with other social bookmarking applications, it is based on the recommendations of real people.

MOG Rolls Out Free On-Demand M Service
Posted 09/19/2011 at 10:16am | by Brad Chacos

More Bookmarking and Tagging Sites

There are a great number of other social bookmarking sites that are worth investigating. A small selection is shown below. Like other applications and websites that appear throughout this book, many of the sites listed below would likely appear in a number of other categories. In the previous pages, we chose to highlight Delicious not because it's necessarily the best product out there but because it is one of the most popular, and so its social content is increasingly enriched by the greater number of people who use it.

9rules	http://www.9rules.com
Blinklist	http://www.blinklist.com
Blogmarks	http://www.blogmarks.net
Blummy	http://www.blummy.com
Bmaccess	http://www.bmaccess.com
Buddymarks	http://www.buddymarks.com
Clipmarks	http://www.clipmarks.com
Connotea	http://www.conotea.org
Diigo	http://www.diigo.com
Feedmarker	http://www.feedmarker.com
HeyStaks	http://www.heystaks.com
Jeteye	http://www.jeteye.com

Knowledge Plaza	http://www.knowledgeplaza.net
Licorizes	http://www.licorizes.com
Mylinkvault	http://www.mylinkvault.com
Onlywire	http://www.onlywire.com
Qoosa	http://www.qoosa.com
Shadows	http://shadows.com
Sitebar	http://www.sitebar.com
Socialmarks	http://www.socialmarks.com
Squidoo	http://www.squidoo.com
Startaid	http://www.startaid.com
Surftail	http://www.surftail.com
Taggle	http://www.taggle.de
Tendango	http://www.tendango.com
Twine	http:///www.twine.com
Yoono	http://www.yoono.com

Cloud Storage

Just as software has begun a slow migration process from desktop to web server, the concept of backing up important data has also shifted in a similar direction. Although it *is* pretty mundane, and certainly at the unglamorous end of the Internet development, data

iCloud, Apple's data hosting system.

hosting is an area of development certain to experience massive growth over the coming years—and is a major part of what frequently has been called "The Cloud." The idea is extremely simple: instead of storing your data on your own media—be it hard drive, CD-R/DVD-R, or memory stick—you upload it to an external server.

Do You Need a Server?

So why, when computer memory seems to be getting cheaper by the day, would you want to back up your data onto someone else's server? The first reason is safety. We've all read the horrible stories about unfortunate people having laptops stolen and losing irreplaceable family photographs that hadn't been backed up. In truth, anyone owning digital content deemed to be of such importance would be advised to keep copies *somewhere* off-site, even it means a stack of DVD-Rs in a drawer at your parents' house. Which brings us to a second reason—reliability. Any professional hosting operation will have its own remote backup server. By using such a service, you *should* be guaranteed that your data is safe.

Depending on how much data you have to store, external hosting can also be a very economical solution. The business model used by most hosting websites entails offering a free service for storing small amounts of data (1–5 gigabytes), and then charging for larger amounts of space or additional services. Many digital image collections will easily fit within these free hosting criteria. If not, with sufficient organizational skill, it would be possible to split a collection over a number of different free hosting services. Musicians or filmmakers, on the other hand, would certainly need to use a paid subscription service to make copies of large audio or video files.

Finally, one increasingly significant reason for using a hosting service is that you can, if desired, share your digital content with others. This is better suited for files that are to be used for collaborative purposes, rather than simply, say, sharing photographs, which can be done more elegantly on a dedicated website like Flickr (*see page 128*). We'll look at the interesting issue of digital collaboration later in the book (*see page 200*).

Box

http://www.box.net

Let's now look at a typical example of a host service. Like most others, Box offers a free service for storing relatively small quantites and charges for using larger amounts of space.

• Begin by entering the URL: **http://www.box.net**.
To open a new account, click on the button marked **Sign Up** on the top right of the menu bar on the main page.

• In the **Signup** window, first select the service plan you wish to use. In this case, we'll select the **Free** service, which allows us to store up to a five gigabytes of

data. Click on the button labeled **Personal**.

• Now enter your registration and login details. Now click on **Continue**. This will take you to a confirmation screen telling you that an e-mail has been sent to you. Reply to the e-mail to complete the registration process.

• When your registration has been verified, click on the button labeled **Login And Get Started**. This will take you to your personal Box.net page (*see below*).

Uploading Files

There are two ways of transferring files from your desktop to the Box.net server. If the file you want is on your desktop, you can simply drag it onto your Box.

net browser homepage; if the file is hidden away in a series of folders, you can use the **Upload** button *(see right)*, which enables you to navigate through your computer's hard drive. Let's look at the drag-and-drop method in more detail.

• Ensure that you're logged into Box.net and are on your home page and that your browser window has been resized so that you have access to the

file you plan to transfer from your desktop. Place the cursor over the file and drag it toward the browser.

• A target box will appear on the browser screen. Drop the file within its borders.

• The progress line indicates how long the transfer will take. When the copy is complete, the name of your file will appear on the screen.

Labeling Your Data

If you have a lot of files loaded into your Box.net account and your file naming methods are less than rigorous, it can be difficult to figure out what information is on a particular file. Box.net allows you to label your files with comments.

• Highlight the file you want to label. Click on the "quote" icon. A text box will appear underneath the file name. Enter any text you want linked to the file and click on the **Add Comment** button. This will then be stored permanently alongside the file.

Tagging Your Data

Like most other data hosting services, Box.net enables its users to apply category tags to their own files. Here's how we can do that.

• Highlight the file you want to label. From the **More Options** drop-down menu (the downward-pointing arrows symbol), select **Add Tags**.

• The **Tags** window will now open. Enter any category tags that you wish to add. Multiple tags should be separated by a comma and a space. If you previously set up categories they will appear in the box below—they can be selected by clicking on the tag name. Click the **OK** button to add your tags. You can use these tags to help you organize your files.

Making Your Files Public

Box.net enables you to take your data into the public domain in two different ways. You can share your files with other Box users and take advantage of features such as social bookmarking tags, or you can simply make them available to anyone with a web browser. Both can be achieved using **More Options** drop-down menu or the **Share** button.

• Highlight the file you want to make public. Click on the **Share** button. The box beneath will appear with a secure URL for downloading the file.

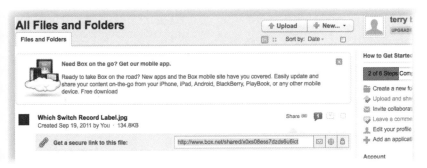

Why Pay?

Given that almost all file sharing websites offer a free basic service for storing 1-5 GB, the question you may well be asking is why you would ever want to take out a paid subscription. If you have very large amounts of data you want to back up in this way, then you may think you have no choice. That is, unless you can easily compartmentalize your activities. It's quite possible, for example, that you might store 5 GB of photographs with one provider; 5 GB of music with a different company; 5 GB of financial documents with another and so forth. It does require discipline to take this approach and in many cases may be more hassle than the money saved taking out a low-cost subscription is worth.

Carbonite

http://www.carbonite.com

Online backup systems represent another recent growth area, of which Carbonite is a fairly typical example. This is not a web-based solution—Carbonite is a piece of software that runs in the background on your computer, automatically copying or updating specified files or file types to a remote server.

The moment you modify or create a new file, the server is updated. Consequently, if you accidentally erase a file or have a drive failure, you can use the software to restore the originals from the server. If you're concerned about security, it isn't possible for your files to be viewed by other users—they are encrypted prior to leaving your computer.

SugarSync

http://www.sugarsync.com

SugarSync is a popular and well-regarded data storage system. Like others it provides free personal storage for small amounts of data and charges for larger volumes. It also enables users to synchronize data with their computers or smart phones and tablets.

OpenDrive

http://www.opendrive.com

OpenDrive offers a free personal account for up to 5GB storage as well as private and public file sharing, direct linking, and online storage. It's also especially well suited to file collaboration. OpenDrive has applications that will run on WIndows and Apple OSX computers and on Apple iPhone formats.

MyPCBackup

http://www.mypcbackup.com

MyPCBackup offers a simple backup system: you install a small piece of software on your PC which periodically backs up your files via the Internet. This system only works with Windows systems.

More Data Hosting Sites

4shared	http://4shared.com	Storegate	http://www.storegate.com
ADrive	http://www.adrive.com	Strongspace	http://www.strongspace.com
ElephantDrive	http://www.elephantdrive.com	TextDrive	http://www.textdrive.com
FlipDrive	http://www.flipdrive.com	Zingee	http://www.zingee.com
Grokthis	http://www.grokthis.net		
Iron Mountain	http://www.ironmountain.com		
Mailbigfile	http://www.mailbigfile.com		
Mozy	http://www.mozy.co.uk		
Multiply	http://multiply.com		
Ourmedia	http://www.ourmedia.org		
Pando	http://www.pando.com		
Railsbase	http://railsbase.com		
Sproutit	http://www.sproutit.com		

Mozy has an online backup plan just your size.

Communications

What is the Internet all about if not communication? There has been a good deal of debate about whether social networking has less to do with communicating with others and is more to do with creating a platform where lone voices can be heard—regardless of there necessarily being an audience. Well, in this section, we will be looking at developments in two-way communication. E-mail, of course, was one of the applications that initially created such a popular buzz in the early days of the Internet. However, two-way online communication can now also include telephone systems, voicemail, links to cell phones, and the bulk transfer of hefty volumes of data. And much of this can be done without paying a cent.

The E-mail Revolution

Since the middle of the 1990s, the widespread use of e-mail has had a truly radical impact on our daily lives. How many of us now even think about communicating by writing hard-copy letters? Why would we do that when we know we can send an e-mail that will arrived at its destination anywhere in the world within a few moments? While a lot of people still use specific e-mail software such as Mail, Outlook, Entourage, Windows Mail, or Eudora, a growing number are now switching to webmail.

E-mail of the Web

Webmail is not a new concept—Windows Live Hotmail, one of the first popular webmail systems, is now over 15 years old. At its most basic, webmail is simply a method of reading and writing e-mails via the Web. This approach does have some significant advantages over using dedicated software. The mail is stored remotely on a server, which means that it is accessible on any computer with an Internet connection and a web browser anywhere in the world. Furthermore, web applications, backups, upgrades, and security are the responsibility of the host. Of course, the user has to be online to read and write mail, which may be a consideration for those who work on the move. As such, many users treat their webmail account as a secondary e-mail system, in addition to traditional desktop-based software.

The prime mover in the world of webmail is, once again, Google. The introduction of the seemingly all-encompassing Gmail has led an ever-growing army of users to abandon their existing e-mail software.

Gmail (Google Mail)

http://www.gmail.com

Gmail—or Google Mail as it is officially known in some parts of the world—is a free AJAX-based webmail and POP3 e-mail service. It was first released as an invitation-only beta application in 2004. The fully functional version was made public in February 2007. As well as offering its own e-mail service, it can also gather mail from up to five other e-mail accounts. Gmail also offers free storage space, so many users will never have to delete archived mails. Every Gmail homepage also has a standard Google search capability.

Setting Up an Account

To create a Gmail account, enter the URL: **http://www.gmail.com**. Click on the button labeled **Create An Account** on the right-hand side of the screen.

• In the account creation page, complete your personal details, including the Gmail login name that will form part of your new e-mail address. When you're happy with this information, click on the button marked: **I Accept. Create My Account**.

• You'll then see your Gmail homepage. This looks and works much like any other e-mail software. For example, if you click on the button marked **Compose Mail**, a blank e-mail page will open up.

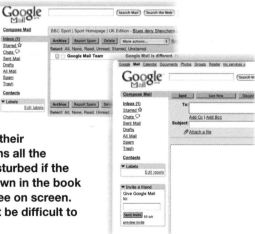

Note: Websites change their design and specifications all the time, so don't be too disturbed if the specific commands shown in the book don't match what you see on screen. Discrepencies shouldn't be difficult to figure out.

Gmail Settings

One of Gmail's most powerful assets is its ability to integrate other e-mail accounts. If, for example, you have several different e-mail addresses for different purposes, you can still access them via your Gmail homepage. So let's look at how you can customize Gmail.

• In your homepage, click on the "cog" symbol on the top right-hand corner of the screen (you'll find it to the right of your user ID). From the drop-down menu click on **Mail Settings**.

• The **Settings** window contains a number of tabbed pages. These equate broadly to the preferences options found in most e-mail software. If you click on the **Accounts and Imports** tab, you can start adding other e-mail addresses to the system.

• Click on the text labeled **Add POP3 Mail Account**. This opens a pop-up window.

• Enter the e-mail address you want to add and then click on the **Next Step button**.

• A second pop-up window opens. Here you must add your POP3 data—typically, username, password, and the name of your POP server.

• Finally, click on the **Add Account** button. When you return to the **Settings and Accounts** window you'll see that the newly entered e-mail address appears on the page. Gmail will now automatically check this account at the same time as checking your Gmail account.

Forwarding Mail to a Cell Phone

If you have a suitably equipped cell phone, you can set Gmail to forward e-mails to your phone. For this to work, your phone must have its own e-mail address, the prefix of which is a ten-digit number. Each service provider has its own domain name for this purpose—Verizon, for example, is vtext.com.

Contact your phone service provider for both of these pieces of data. (This feature may not be possible in some countries outside the United States.)

• In the **Settings** window, click on the tab marked **Forwarding and POP**. In the Forwarding section, enter your phone's e-mail address. Click on the **Save Changes** button. Gmail will now automatically forward e-mails to your cell phone.

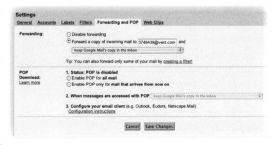

This really does just scratch the surface of what's possible with Gmail. You'd be well advised to take a look at the various FAQs that Google has created to this end: **http://mail.google.com/mail/help/about.html** is a good place to start.

Google's April Fools' Pranks

Although its founders are among America's wealthiest entrepreneurs, Google's origins as a university research project occasionally resurface with bursts of geeky humor. In fact, Google usually now makes some kind of announcement to the world on April Fools' Day.

In 2002, Google came up with PigeonRank, a parody of its own PageRank system. The press release claimed that clusters of pigeons could be used to rank webpages faster than human editors or machine-based algorithms and that PigeonRank provided the basis for all Google's web search tools.

In 2004, job ads were placed for Google's Copernicus Center, a ficticious research facility on the moon. The project was the development of a new operating system called Luna/X—a pun on Linux, with a logo that looked remarkably like Windows XP.

In 2007, Google changed the Gmail login page to announce a new service called Gmail Paper. This offered users of the service the opportunity to add e-mails to a "paper archive," which Google would print and return via more traditional postal means.

In 2011, Google claimed to be introducing a service called Gmail Motion that would allowed users to navigate e-mails, send, and even dictate messages through the user's physical actions captured on a webcam. To send an e-mail, for example, the user would perform the action of licking a stamp and posting it! After the user signed up, they would be directed to an "April Fools'" message.

The company has also announced genuine products on April Fools' Day. This marketing strategy has been used to make people think that a product is a hoax, spread the word virally, and then create publicity when it becomes clear that it is real. Gmail itself was announced in this way. Since at that time (2004) a free e-mail service that featured one gigabyte of storage space was unheard of, it looked quite like a feasible hoax.

Telephone and Messaging

One of the reasons for the growing popularity of Internet-based live communications systems is that they are cheap—or even free—to use. It's true that peer-to-peer voice and video systems have existed in the past, but they have now migrated from a technical user base toward those for whom computers have traditionally offered little in the way of allure. So let's take a look at some of the most popular of these applications.

Skype

http://www.skype.com

Skype is a peer-to-peer telephone network system developed by Niklas Zennström and Janus Friis—the duo that were also behind the file-sharing application Kazaa. The beta version of Skype was made available in 2003, and within two years its success was such that it was acquired by the eBay company. Skype's first wave of popularity came from the fact that any two suitably equipped individuals, anywhere in the world, could talk across the Internet for no cost at all. Users were required to have a computer fitted with a microphone, speaker, and broadband Internet connection. Later, Skype evolved to incorporate moving images, so users with webcam-equipped computers could use it as a videophone system. As a business model, unlike many others operating in the field of technology, Skype has been able to evolve successfully with the introduction of a number of paid services—for example, calls from computers to landline phones. By 2011 there were estimated to be over 600 million Skype users worldwide. That same year Microsoft paid $8.5 billion for full ownership of the company.

Installing Skype

Unlike most of the applications in this book, Skype is a piece of stand-alone software that runs on your computer. So the first stage is to download and install Skype on your computer.

• Enter the URL **http://www.skype.com** into your browser. In the menu bar at the top of the screen, click on **Get Skype**. From the drop-down menu, choose the system and operation system you use. This one is for Apple Mac.

• Skype offers both a free system and the commercial Skype Premium option. Here we will download the free version. Click on **Download Skype**.

Skype is compatible with the vast majority of operating systems: OSX for Apple Macintosh; IOS for Apple iPads and iPods; Android; Windows; Linux. It also works with a number of Sony, Panasonic, and Samsung televisions. The example above shows the download screen and four simple steps for installing Skype onto an Apple Macintosh; Windows users launch the downloaded Skype Installer and follow the steps within the **Setup Wizard**; Linux users can follow the Skype download instructions from the home screen; IOS users can download the free Skype App from the **iTunes App Store**; Android users can obtain the free app from Google's **Android Market**.

To launch the Skype program in Apple OSX, click on the application icon—opening the software using the other platforms can be done in a broadly similar manner.

Using Skype

Here are the simple steps you need to follow to make telephone calls using Skype. Regular Skype calls—those made to other computers—are free of charge, even if you are at opposite ends of the world. Smartphones armed with the Skype app connected via a wifi broadband link are also free to use. You can make Skype calls from your computer to a regular land telephone, although these are charged.

• Launch the Skype application. In the welcome screen you are asked to enter your **Skype Name** and **Password**, and then click on **Sign In**. If you haven't yet registered, click on the button labeled **Create New Account**.

• In the **Create a New Account** window, enter the name you want to use as your Skype identity, a password, and an e-mail address. Finally, click on the **Create** button. This will take you back to the welcome screen, but with your details automatically entered. Click on the **Sign In** button. Skype will open.

Let's begin by adding a contact for you to call.

• From the **Contacts** menu, choose **Add Contact**.

• The **Add Contact** window appears. Enter the name of the contact you wish to add, and then click on the **Find** button.

• Skype will now create a list of people of the name you entered. Highlight the correct entry in the list and click on the green **Add** symbol on the right of the row.

• A new window will pop up. This sends an immediate online notice to the person in question, asking them if they would be happy for you to see when they are online. If they agree, you will receive a confirmation notice, and their name will appear in your list of contacts on the left of the main Skype screen.

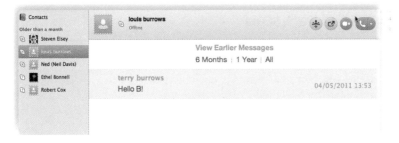

Using Skype

To begin making a call, highlight the Skype Name on left hand side of your main screen. It will open out to include any public profile information that your contact has set up. To make the call, click on the green telephone symbol found on the right of the window.

• A window headed **Connecting . . .** will pop up. If your contact has set up a profile, including an image, this will appear in this window.

• When your contact answers, a new pop-up window will appear. If he or she has a webcam attached, you will be able to see that person while they are talking to you. If you both have webcams, your own video image will appear in a small box in the corner of the window.

• To end the call, click on the red telephone button in the corner of the window.

Internet Phone Tips

Many modern laptop computers feature in-built camera, microphone, and loudspeakers, meaning that everything you need to make calls of Skype, or other such systems, is already in place. One important consideration, though, is of sound quality. When making Internet phone calls you can easily experience unpleasant feedback or echo effects. This happens when the sound from the loudspeaker is picked up by the microphone and then retransmitted back to the caller, which is then transmitted back to you. This can be avoided to some degree by controlling the volume of your speakers. Another simple solution which will prevent this problem altogether is to channel the sound through a pair of earphones. If you intend to make frequent calls this way, a worthwhile investment would be a USB-connected headset—with the microphone directly in front of your mouth, the other party will not hear so much of the often "boomy" room acoustics, which can sometimes make it difficult to hear what's being said.

Instant Messaging with Skype

In addition to making Internet telephone calls, Skype also allows for online text messaging. It works in much the same way as making a telephone call.

• Highlight the name of your chosen contact, and click on the "word bubble" on the far right of the window.

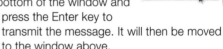

• The chat window will now pop up. To send a text message, type in the panel at the bottom of the window and press the Enter key to transmit the message. It will then be moved to the window above.

• Any replies to your message will appear in the window, each message appearing on a separate line.

It's not strictly necessary for the other party to be connected in order to send Skype text messages. You can send your note and the other party will receive it next time they log in—much in the same way as a text message on a cell phone or even a traditional e-mail.

Meebo

http://www.meebo.com

The true value of any communications system comes down to one basic question. Are enough of the people you want to talk to using the same system? And if not, are the different systems compatible? This is where Meebo comes in. Through the main Meebo website you can access all of the major instant messaging systems—AIM, Yahoo!, Google Talk, MSN, ICQ, and Jabber—from a single portal. Individual chats take place in pop-up windows that you can then move around the screen. Meebo is a very neat system if you have a number of different online lives on different online chat networks.

• Enter the URL: **http://www. meebo.com**. Begin by setting up a Meebo account and password. Once you've done that, simply enter the ID and passwords for all of your instant messaging accounts, and then click on the **Sign On** button.

Once you have registered, the first screen will ask you to you choose which messaging systems you want to be able to access from Meebo. When you have your selection, click on the **Finish** button.

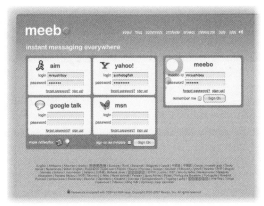

In this example, we have set up accounts for the AOL Instant Messenger (AIM) and Yahoo! Messenger. The main page can also accommodate Google Talk, MSN, Facebook, Jabber, Flixster, Xomba, Ustream,

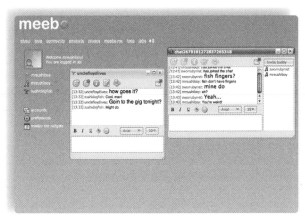

Bebo, and numerous other networks.

Your Meebo homepage lists the active messengers on the left of the screen. Whenever a new IM comes your way, a new box will pop up in the window. Meebo uses a generic chat window regardless of which messenger is being used—you type your message at the foot of the screen and then press the **Enter** key to transmit—the running conversation will appear in the top half of the window.

Meebo Widget

Meebo also has a feature known as Meebo Me. This is a small chat window that can be inserted into any webpage—enabling visitors to chat with you. To set it up, click on **Meebo Me** on the menu bar. Name your window, add your ID and password, and Meebo will automatically generate the html code, which you can then copy and paste into your own chosen website.

Sending Data

In the past, if we wanted to transfer data files via the Internet, we would simply send an e-mail with an attachment. And for small files, this is still probably the simplest solution. However, most ISPs place some kind of upper limit on file sizes, and even if they don't, many company firewalls will prevent e-mails with large attachments from reaching their destinations. One solution is to use an FTP (File Transfer Protocol) system. However, most nonbusiness users don't have easy access to such facilities. A modern solution has come through a number of web-based solutions. Let's look at one of the most widely used data transmission websites—YouSendIt.

YouSendIt

http://www.yousendit.com

Founded in 2003, YouSendIt is a temporary file-hosting website. The user uploads data files to the site along with the e-mail addresses of the proposed recipients. YouSendIt then forwards an e-mail to those addresses with a download link back to the file. Files are deleted after a week or a specific number of downloads. It markets itself as an alternative to sending large e-mail attachments. The company offers different levels of service—simple transfers of files up to 50 MB in size are free, but monthly charges are levied for greater sizes or quantities. For example, YouSendIt Pro allows for 2GB files to be sent anytime for a subscription cost of less than $50 per year.

• Enter the URL: **http://www.yousendit. com**. Follow the registration instructions.

• To send a file, enter the e-mail addresses of the recipients and optional subject matter and message text. Click on Select File to browse your desktop for the file you wish to transfer. Click on the **Send It** button. Both you and the recipient will receive e-mails once the file has been uploaded. The e-mail gives the receiver a link from which the file can then be downloaded.

Other E-mail Applications

Many of the larger domain-hosting organizations offer their own webmail services. Since these are linked directly to the domain servers, it could be argued that they are likely to be faster and more reliable than a third party. Not all of the sites mentioned below are free.

BigString	http://www.bigstring.com	LavaBit	http://www.lavabit.com
BlueTie	http://www.bluetie.com	LuxSci	http://www.luxsci.com
ContactOffice	http://www.contactoffice.com	MSN Hotmail	http://www.hotmail.com
FastMail	http://www.fastmail.fm	MyWay	http://www.myway.com
InBox	http://www.inbox.com	Yahoo! Mail	http://www.yahoo.com

Other Telephone Applications

There's a growing market for Internet phones that operate without a computer but still communicate through a broadband connection. A number of the companies below operate in this field. They are worth looking into since they generally represent a far better financial deal than those offered by the traditional telecommunications organizations. The downside is that quality of sound and reliability of connection may not always match up to those of conventional landlines.

8x8	http://www.packet8-voip.com	Ooma	http://www.ooma.com
BroadVoice	http://www.broadvoice.com	Radvision	http://www.radvision.com
FWD	http://www.freeworlddialup.com	RingCentral	http://www.ringcentral.com
HamSphere	http://www.hamsphere.com	SunRocket	http://www.sunrocket.com
Lingo	http://www.lingo.com	VoiceWing	http://www.verizon.com
Mediacom	http://www.mediacomcc.com	Vonage	http://www.vonage.com

Other Instant Messaging Applications

These are all dedicated instant messaging websites. Most of them are accessible using Meebo as a portal.

Aim	https://www.aim.com	Jabber	http://www.jabber.com
Blauk	http://www.blauk.com	MSN	http://www.msn.com
EBuddy	http://www.ebuddy.com	MXit	http://www.mxit.com
Google Talk	http://www.google.com	VZOchat	http://wwwvzochat.com
Gadu-Gadu	http://www.gadugadu.com	Xfire	http://www.xfire.com
ICQ	http://www.icq.com	Yahoo! Messenger	http://www.messenger.yahoo.com

Other File-Transfer Applications

All of the applications shown below offer a basic free service—the sort that would satisfy most nonbusiness users. But for larger files, more frequent transmissions, or more recipients, there will be charges.

DropBox	http://www.dropbox.com	Sendspace	http://www.sendspace.com
Dropsend	http://www.dropsend.com	Tempinbox	http://www.tempinbox.com
Myemail	http://myemail.com	Trustmymail	http://www.trustmymail.com

Design

This segment of the book is all about applications that aim to aid the design process—among them, tools to help web designers or graphics sites that are just fun to use.

Clickdensity

http://www.clickdensity.com

As websites become increasingly important to business, and greater numbers compete with one another for user attention, design efficiency becomes more and more significant.

Clickdensity is an analytical tool that enables web administrators to get a greater feel for how their sites are being used. In essence, Clickdensity provides a "heat map," showing concentration of mouse movements on your website. This can be based on mouse clicks or simply where the mouse has been rolled. So not only do you gain an understanding of where your audience's attention is being focused, but also where it is *not*. Hence "dead" space can be identified.

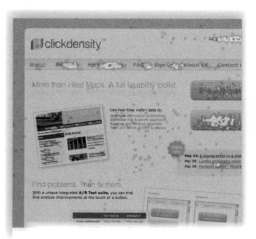

The visual nature of the Clickdensity display makes it particularly good for presentations to nontechnical audiences, such as marketing executives.

Flickrlogomakr

http://flickr.nosv.org

This website produces a Flickr-style logo. Simply type in the text and click on the **Make** button. The graphic can then be downloaded.

LogoSauce

http://www.logosauce.com

For amateur web designers and owners of small businesses, the subject of a logo can be a troublesome one. Coming up with the right design and suitable typography takes skill—and if you get it wrong your business identity can be affected. LogoSauce is an online catalog of cutting-edge logo design. It allows anyone to see at a glance what the prevailing fashions are within the industry. Users are also able to make comments on designs.

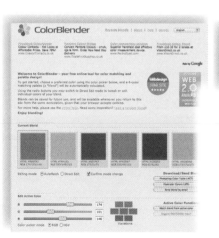

ColorBlender

http://www.colorblender.com

Color matching is obviously a critical skill for most designers. ColorBlender is a web-based tool used for creating palettes in web design. By choosing a single base color, a complementary blend of six matching colors are shown, each with its own HTML and RGB blends. Thus, a complete color scheme can be chosen simply.

Picreflect

http://www.picreflect.com

A useful webtool, especially for those who don't have access to professional design software such as Photoshop, Picreflect allows you to upload a photograph, rescale it, rotate the image, add reflection effects, and add degrees of transparency.

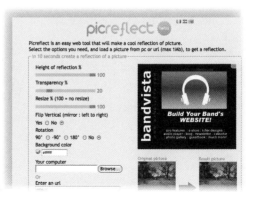

Typetester

http://www.typetester.maratz.com

The skill of the typographer is often overlooked in design. Selecting a font that is both attractive and readable, however, is a critical to the success of any kind of book, magazine, or website design.

Typetester is an extremely useful web-based application that allows users to test out different styles and combinations of text, with the results being immediately visible.

It's very simple to use: you select a typeface (called a "font") from one of the drop-down menus. Directly beneath that are a number of other variables that can be manipulated, such the size of the print, the leading (the space between each line),

tracking (the space between each letter), and alignment, as well as foreground and background colors. You can immediately see your changes reflected in the dummy "lorem ipsum" text beneath each column. Typetester allows three different settings to be shown on the screen at the same time, thus allowing direct comparisons to be made between each one.

Resizr

http://resizr.lord-lance.com

Simple tool for resizing images, either from the web or on your desktop. You load an image and drag the slider to alter the dimensions. The proportions remain in place.

Flower Maker

http://www.zefrank.com/flowers

This application is enjoyable for wasting a few idle moments. The sole purpose of Flower Maker is, as its name suggests, to create images of flowers. On the left of the screen you'll see a variety of petal shapes and a color palette: click on your chosen color and petal, and drag the

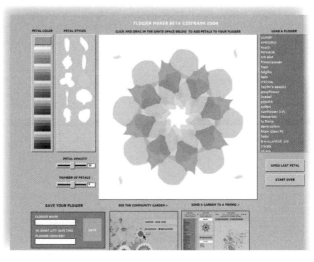

mouse in the whiteboard area. You will see that it creates a pleasant kaleidoscopic effect. You can continue to add more petals.

Pixenate

http://www.pixenate.com

Having seen already that there are passable web-based alternatives to the big guns of office software, it comes as no surprise to find that there are also plenty of free-to-use image manipulation applications to be found. Pixenate is capable of performing some of the basic functions of popular (and costly) desktop applications such as Adobe Photoshop. After you have uploaded an image you can zoom in and out, crop, rotate, or perform simple color alterations, such as altering contrast and brightness or fixing red eye. Finished photographs can then be uploaded to Flickr.

e-Commerce

Whether buying or selling, the Internet, and in particular the World Wide Web, has altered the way many of us do business. In some areas—notably CDs, books, and DVDs—online sales make up an increasingly significant proportion of the total. And to help our sales transactions go through more safely and smoothly, Internet-based currencies such as PayPal have now become universally accepted.

eBay
http://www.ebay.com

One of the global commercial successes of the past decade, the online auction website eBay was founded in 1995 in San Jose, California, by computer programmer Pierre Omidyar. The first item purportedly sold on eBay was a broken laser pointer, which sold for $14.83. (The oft-repeated story that eBay was founded to help his fiancée trade PEZ dispensers was fabricated by a PR company to generate media interest.) The website flourished at an astonishing speed, and when eBay went public in September 1997, it made Omidyar an overnight billionaire.

Although eBay first came to prominence as a means for auctioning used goods, its focus has slowly shifted to the point where a significant proportion of items on sale are now brand-new. Thus, for many customers now, eBay is viewed less as a place to go to find a second-hand bargain than simply as the world's biggest online store.

Finding Products on eBay

Almost anything you care to imagine—and we mean *anything* (see the box across the page)—is likely to be available somewhere in the world on eBay.

• Begin by entering eBay's URL: **http://www.ebay.com**. In this example, we'll see if we can find anyone selling a Ford Mustang car. Enter **Mustang** in the box at the top of the page and click on the **Search** button.
• The list covers any item that

Famous eBay Sales
• Fed up with his whole life, Australian Ian Usher decided to sell it on eBay. The winning bidder, who paid around £192,000, received the man's house, car, job, and introductions to his friends.
• In May 2005, a Volkswagen Golf that had previously been owned by Cardinal Ratzinger (who had just been elected Pope Benedict XVI) was sold on eBay's German site for 188,938.88 Euros.
• A man from Arizona sold an air guitar on eBay.com for $5.50.
• Disney sold a decommissioned monorail for $20,000.
• The German Language Association auctioned the German language to call attention to the growing influence of Pidgin-English in modern German.
• In November 2005, the original Hollywood sign was sold on eBay for $450,400.
• A student from Coventry, UK, sold a single corn flake for just over $2.
• Producers on the TV show *Ally McBeal* once used eBay to auction a walk-on part.
• An old lunch box containing a decade-old cheese sandwich, on which mold had formed in the shape of the face of Virgin Mary, was sold for $28,000.

has the word "Mustang" in its title. If we look at the column headed **Matching Categories** and then click on **Cars & Trucks** the list will be filtered.

• The list then reduces to only items in the **Cars & Trucks** category. If you want to find detailed information on one of the items, click on the title of the auction.

• If you want to bid for the item, click on the button marked **Place Bid**. (Note: you have be signed in to your eBay account to bid for an item.) Enter your maximum bid and click on the **Continue** button.

Selling Items on eBay

To sell an item on eBay you first must be registered and signed into your eBay account.

• On the main page, click on the **Sell** button in the top right corner of the screen. From the drop-down menu select **Sell An Item**.

• There are different ways you can set up your auction. One of the easiest methods is to use the search feature, which automatically identifies the relevant sales category. This is much faster than working it out manually. In the **Sell** window, type in some key words that describe the item. Here we'll try to sell a car—enter **Austin Allegro** and click on the **Start Selling** button.

• Based on your search, eBay will come up with some possible categories. These will be based on what others have used for similar items. In this example, in the checkbox click on **Cars, Vans & Vehicles > Classic Cars > Austin**. Click on the button marked **Save and Continue**.

• Now that eBay understands that it's a car you're selling, it presents you with a specific template. Complete the details, write your sales blurb, upload a photograph, and then review your listing. When you're ready, click on the **List Your Item** button.

Your listing is now set up and can be viewed by anyone. You can check out bidding by looking at your **My eBay** page, which lists everything that you are bidding for and selling.

Tips for Selling on eBay

Good feedback At the very heart of eBay is the feedback system, which allows buyers and sellers to rate one another after transactions. If you have a feedback rating of 100%, and a large number of transactions behind you, it means that everyone on eBay with whom you've had dealings has been satisfied with the way you carried out your business. This means you are likely to be viewed as tristworthy in the eyes of potential customers.

Good image People like to see things before they buy them. Make sure any products you list on eBay are accompanied by good quality photographs.

Research Spend some time researching other similar products and following the bidding process.

Shipping Make sure that you include the shipping costs on your listing.

Details Prepare a powerful listing. The trick is to combine phrasing that will work for a search engine with concrete details about the product that will entice people to bid.

Payments Offer a full complement of payment options. Many eBayers prefer to use PayPal, so make sure that you set up an account.

Act professionally Provide the kind of customer service that will build your reputation and feedback ratings.

Auction Mapper

http://www.auctionmapper.com

An independent website, Auction Mapper is a more attractive way to find items on eBay. Users enter their search criteria, then Auction Mapper looks at what is currently available on eBay and places the results on a Google map.

• Enter the URL—**http//www. auctionmapper.com**. In the home page enter your zip code and the item for which you want to search. Here we'll enter a Manhattan zip and do a search for a Fender Telecaster guitar. Click on **Go!**

• You'll see a map of the United States, and a list of categories in which your search has been found. Choose a category, drag it and drop it on the map. You will now see a map of the New York City area on which the auction locations have been marked.

PayPal

http://www.paypal.com

PayPal is the virtual currency at the heart of the Internet. The company came about in 2000, the result of a merger of two smaller online credit organizations. Its success is largely linked to that of eBay, who, two years later, acquired the company. While PayPal had a number of competitors, most have since conceded defeat and closed down.

Registered users place funds in a PayPal account, or provide credit card details against which funds can be drawn. This enables small businesses or those selling items on eBay (or other auction sites) to accept credit card payments without undergoing the punitive costs associated with creating an account with a credit organization. Accounts are free to create, but charges are applied to individual transactions. For regular eBay sellers, having a PayPal account is now seen as a basic necessity.

Amazon

http://www.amazon.com

Amazon is probably the world's best-known online retailer—it's certainly the most commercially successful. It started out in 1994 selling just books, then gradually spread into other areas, such as CDs, DVDs, toys, and electrical goods. Although the company itself predates such ideas as The Cloud and Web 2.0 by many years, it falls under this umbrella because of its early social networking/blogging features. In this example let's look for a book about how to read music.

• Type in **http://www.amazon.com**. This will produce a list of books matching your search criteria. Scroll down the list until you see a book that looks as if it might fit the bill.

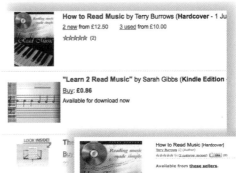

• By clicking on the title you can find out more detail about the book on its own unique Amazon page. As well as information on pricing and availability, sometimes it can feature sample pages for you to view. If you want to buy the book, click on the **Add to Basket** icon on the right of the screen. When you've finished shopping, click on **Proceed to Checkout** and follow the instructions.

Amazon quickly saw the value of enabling its customers to make comments on the things they'd bought. A good set of reviews for a book by a little-known author definitely has an impact on sales. So much so, in fact, that there have been well-publicized stories about purportedly independent comments actually coming from book publishers, agents, or authors themselves.

More e-Commerce Sites

AboutUs.org	http://www.aboutus.org	Flyspy	http://www.flyspy.com
Adgenta	http://www.adgenta.com	Fundable	http://www.fundable.com
Ansearch	http://www.ansearch.com	Gumshoo	http://www.gumshoo.com
Bigcartel	http://bigcartel.com	Hawkee	http://www.hawkee.com
Billmonk	https://www.billmonk.com	Oolsi	http://www.oolsi.com
Blish	http://www.blish.com	Qoop	http://www.qoop.com
Castingwords	http://castingwords.com	Smarkets	http://www.smarkets.com
Cafépress	http://www.cafepress.com	Starting Point Directory	http://www.stp.com
Carbonmade	http://www.carbonmade.com	Stylehive	http://www.shopify.com
Clipfire	http://www.clipfire.com	Wazima	http://www.wazima.com
Cooqy	http://www.cooqy.com	Wists	http://www.wists.com
Coverpop	http://www.coverpop.com	Yelp	http://www.yelp.com
Donorschoose	http://www.donorschoose.org	Yub	http://www.yub.com
Etsy	http://www.etsy.com	Zopa	http://www.zopa.com

Education and Knowledge

There has been much discussion about democracy on the Internet—especially in regard to the access to and sharing of knowledge and information. In fact, this interchange goes back the earliest days of the Internet when specialist "Usernet" newsgroups were used as forums for answering questions. While newsgroups still have many users, the most interesting developments have long shifted the web, where more recent technologies like AJAX have allowed for the creation of slick, easy-to-use interfaces. Here is a selection of knowledge-based, user-enriched websites.

7 Tips On

http://www.7tipson.com

7 Tips lists simple, single-sentence hints and tips posted by its users. Tips can be tagged and searched for in a variety of ways—the main screen features a cloud of the most popular tags; alternatively, a conventional text search can be used. There is a wide range of responses, from the highly practical to the extremely silly, and it's a surprisingly addictive website.

Answers.com

Answers.com

http://www.answers.com

Launched in 1999, Answers.com is a well-established information site, drawing on a variety of different sources on the Internet—although strongly geared toward Wikipedia. At the start of 2011, the owners of the site claimed that it had provided over 11 million answers in total.

MetaGlossary

http://www.metaglossary.com

MetaGlossary is a neat dictionary of user-defined terms, phrases, and acronyms. Enter a phrase in the main window and click on the button marked **Define**. A new window opens containing any definitions posted by other users. Over 2 million such definitions have been compiled.

Askville

http://www.askville.com

Owned by Amazon, Askville is a question and answer website. Unlike other similar services, however, Askville makes use of gaming features. For example, users gain or lose "experience points" for their expertise in specific topics depending on the quality of their answers. Askville also has a vibrant social community, driven by the site's discussion boards, where "Askvillians" are able to enter into lengthy debate sparked by individual questions. In 2009, the Askville Awards were initiated as a way of both rewarding its active members and motivating newer recruits.

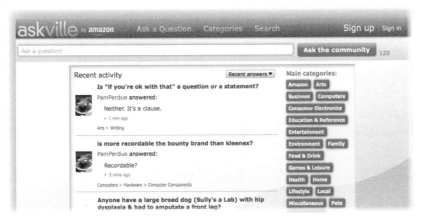

Quotiki

http://www.quotiki.com

If you've ever tried to remember a quotation, who said it, or the precise wording, Quotiki could

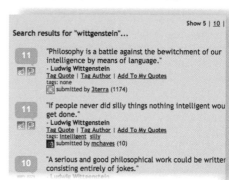

be just the website for you. It's very simple to use: in the single search box near the top of the window, you can enter either a word, name, or an extract from a phrase. Let's take an example, typing **Wittgenstein** in the search box. If you now click on the **Search** button, you will see a selection of quotes by the noted philosopher.

Squidoo

http://www.squidoo.com

Launched in 2005 by book publisher Seth Godin, Squidoo is a network of what it calls user-generated lenses. These are single pages of information that can be written on any subject. Squidoo relies on advertising and affiliate links to create revenue, half of which goes to the writers—or "lensmasters." Nearly half of their shared earnings are donated to charities. In 2010, the company donated an additional $275,000 to charity. By the end of 2010, Squidoo had over 1.5 million hand-built lenses.

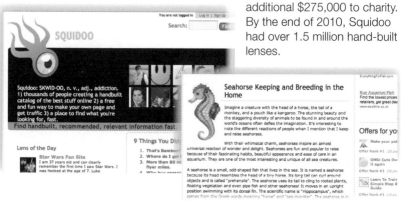

Yahoo! Answers

http://answers.yahoo.com

By far the largest website of its kind, Yahoo! Answers describes itself as "a community-driven knowledge market." It was launched at the end of 2005, and within a year was able to boast over 65 million answers and more than 7 million questions. Although based in the United States, there are international sites devoted to most major countries and languages. Several notable figures have appeared on Yahoo! Answers to ask questions, among them Hillary Clinton and Barack Obama.

Answerbag

http://www.answerbag.com

Founded in 2003 by Joel Downs, Answerbag is now the second most widely used Q&A website, after Yahoo! Answers. It works in much the same way: questions are posted and answered by the community.

More Education and Knowledge Sites

3Form	http://3form.org	Jots	http://www.jots.com
Askeet	http://www.askeet.com	Manage My Ideas	http://www.managemyideas.com
Brainreactions	http://www.brainreactions.net	Nuvvo	http://www.nuvvo.com
Bubbl.us	http://bubbl.us	ProProfs	http://www.proprofs.com
Copyscape	http://www.copyscape.com	Quomon	http://quomon.com
Echosign	http://www.echosign.com/public/compose	Root/vaults	http://www.root.net/vaults
Gibeo	http://www.gibeo.net	Sparkhive	http://www.sparkhive.com
GuruLib	http://www.gurulib.com	Tractis	http://www.tractis.com
Hanzoweb	http://hanzoarchives.com	WisdomDB	http://www.wisdomdb.net
Helium	http://www.helium.com	Wondir	http://www.wondir.com

eHow

http://www.ehow.com

An excellent source of basic information covering a diverse range of subject matter, from acne to zoology. This is not a wiki-type site to which anyone can contribute; articles are written specifically for eHow by experts. Let's look at the type of thing on offer.

• Enter the eHow URL, which is **http://www.ehow.com**.

• Click on **Explore Topics** from the menu bar at the top of the screen.

• Let's now look into one of the categories on offer: Click on the text labeled **Art History**.

• This category is split into more sections, including specific tabs for artists, styles, and major works of art. On the main page there is a trailer for an article called **Cubism 101**. Click on the title text.

• This takes us to the first part the article we wanted to read, which was **Cubism: Art Histoy 101 Basics**.

HubPages

http://www.hubpages.com

Launched in 2006 with a $2 million investment, HubPages is a user generated content site. "Hubbers," as the content-providers are known, submit magazine-style articles which are posted as individual webpages, or "hubs." The appeal to the "everyday experts" (as its contributers are described on the

site) is that any income derived from advertisements is split 60:40 between the site and the author. Authors are encouraged to allow comments on their articles, and also to respond to them.

Recognized in 2010 as one of the year's "Hottest Silicon Valley Companies," HubPages is one of the 50 most visited US websites—in December 2010, it received over 40 million visits.

How Stuff Works

http://www.howstuffworks.com

A simple idea, as the name would suggest, experts attempt to explain simply how all kinds of diferent things function.

Games and Virtual Worlds

During the first half of the 1980s, when personal computers first became affordable to domestic users, many people bought them expecting to be able to do useful things, such as managing their accounts; most ended up using them for one thing, and one thing only—playing games. Unsurprisingly, perhaps, computer gaming of some sort has been in existence almost since the birth of the computer. Much of this activity took place within the confines of university research labs, and it wasn't until the development of the microprocessor, which would in turn make possible the invention of the personal computer, that computer gaming reached the public. As computers and their graphics capabilities have become more powerful, so have the games become more sophisticated, enabling the creation of "virtual worlds" with a potential limited only by the imagination of the players. In this section, we'll take a brief look at the history of the computer game and at a selection of those available either via the web or as free downloaded software.

Background to Computer Gaming

There seems to be no unequivocal agreement as to when the first computer game appeared. One of the most commonly cited candidates is Spacewar!, developed by students at MIT in 1961. The game consisted of two player-controlled spaceships maneuvering around a central star, each attempting to destroy the other. It was designed for use on a PDP-1 computer, a machine intended for number-crunching statistical calculations.

The first generation of personal computers saw the evolution of text-based interactive adventure gaming, in which the player controlled characters by entering commands through a keyboard. The first such popular title, Adventure, was developed in 1972. During the explosion of growth in the 1980s, adventure games were still among the most popular, but, as CPU power began to increase dramatically, graphics started to take a more prominent role. Furthermore, as the mouse became an increasingly standard piece of hardware on personal computers, its use was gradually adopted in more and more games.

In 1991, the first first-person shooter game appeared—Hovertank 3D—which represented the first use of real-time 3D graphics. The same producer went on to develop Wolfenstein 3D a year later, which is widely viewed as having kick-started the biggest-selling genre of modern times. The PC release of Doom in 1993 represented a major breakthrough in computer gaming, providing players with a 3D experience of unprecedented realism. Since then, in terms of content, the games themselves have not changed massively: what continues to evolve at a startling rate is the quality of the 3D graphics.

To a large degree, developments over the last decade have taken place away from the pesonal computer and have shifted to dedicated gaming units, such as the PlayStation series, XBox, and various Nintendo products. One exception has been the growth of virtual world games, which take place either via a web browser or dedicated software linked to a network of players via a fast Internet connection. The most famous example of this is Second Life, a world where it's possible to buy virtual property, build houses, and buy products—"real" or otherwise—from virtual stores.

Web 2.0 Games

http://www.ajaxgames.blogspot.com

This is as good a place to start as any—Web 2.0 Games is a directory site/blog that enables users to make links and comment on games that have been designed using what could be described as "Web 2.0 technology." More broadly, the intention here is to highlight games that have been created using AJAX or similar technologies.

The main page consists of two elements. On the right of the screen is a scrolling list of games—you click on the name of the game to link to its website. On the left of the screen is blog information about such games entered by users. Let's try an example.

• Enter the URL: **http://www.ajaxgames.blogspot.com**. From the list of games on the right click on **Kdice**.

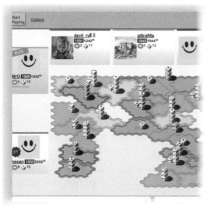

• The AJAX game Kdice opens up. This is a multiplayer interactive strategy game based on the popular online Dice Wars—itself a variation on the board game Risk, where players seek to control all territories on the map. The other players currently online can be seen dotted around the edges of the board.

• To begin, click on the button marked **Start Playing**.

Second Life

http://www.secondlife.com

Second Life has quite simply been *the* phenomenon of the online virtual world. Founded in 2003 by Linden Research, Inc., it uses a downloadable client program to create a network where users (often termed "Residents" or "Lifers") are able to interact with one another in a surreal, three-dimensional world. Each participant has a graphic representation, or avatar, within Second Life. Initially, he or she chooses from a number of human likenesses and dress styles. These can later be altered dramatically, or new looks can be purchased from virtual stores.

Second Life (or "SL," as it is commonly known) was by no means the first virtual world, and not even the most widely inhabited—that would arguably be the online version of The Sims. SL is noteworthy for having created such an advanced level of social networking. Residents can explore, socialize, participate in individual and group activities, and even create and trade items (virtual property) and services with one another. There are over six million registered users, although many of these are thought to be inactive.

Second Life was inspired by the cyberpunk literary movement of the 1980s, particularly novels of William Gibson and Neal Stephenson. Indeed, the stated goal of Linden was to create a place like the Metaverse described in Stephenson's novel *Snow Crash*—a user-defined world of general use in which people interacted, played, and conducted business. To this end, SL developed a virtual currency, the Linden Dollar (L$), which is exchangeable in the "real" world for US dollars—this rate fluctuates like any other currency market but is usually somewhere between L$270–300 to a single US dollar. But business is no joke in Second Life: there are a handful of Lifers earning in excess of US

$200,000 a year from trading activities within Second Life.

Although a virtual world, there are numerous "real-world" bodies existing within Second Life. The Maldives, Sweden, and Estonia all have completely serious, legitimate government embassies there. Furthermore, a number of churches and universities maintain a practical presence.

So What's the Point in Second Life?

SL is not a computer game as such, since there is no scoring system, nobody gets

killed, and there are no winners or losers—indeed, Lifers tend to resent their universe being described in such a way. Perhaps it's best thought of as a game in the sense more traditionally played by small children, where activities are played out with little more in mind than enjoyment in its own right.

It's fair to say that some Lifers take their virtual lives very seriously. Indeed, there have been plenty of articles and news stories that have documented the problems of Second Life "addicts" whose connection to their computer worlds have caused them considerable problems in the "real" world.

Getting Started
Second Life has such depth that we can only really scratch the surface within a few pages. So let's take a look at how to get started.

• Begin by entering the URL: **http://www.secondlife.com**. To set up your account, click on the **Join Now** button.

• In the registration page, enter a **First Name** of your own choice and then click on the drop-down menu to choose a **Last Name** from the options provided. Enter your **Birthdate** and an **E-mail Address**. Click on the button marked **Continue**.

Creating Your Avatar
Now select your basic avatar. Choose one of the options—you'll see a full-size image alongside when you click on any button. When you're ready, click on **Choose This Avatar**.

Second Life Registration: Basic Details

Choose Your Second Life Name

Your Second Life name is your unique in-world identity. You're able to create your own first name and select from a wide variety of last names. Please choose your Second Life name carefully, since it can't be changed later.

First name: Rlyst   Last name: Lundquist
2-31 characters, numbers and letters only

Check this name for availability

Enter Your Birthdate

Please provide an accurate birthdate for your own protection. We ask your birthdate to verify your account. If you ever forget your Second Life name or password.

Month: January   Day: 11   Year: 1969
(ex: 1980)

Enter Your Email Address

Please use a real email address. We need it to send you an account activation link. We won't give it out to anyone without your explicit permission.

Email: sushiboy@sushiboy.com
Enter again for verification: sushiboy@sushiboy.com

(Continue)

Select an Avatar

Welcome, Illy Lundquist!

Next step is to choose the way you want to look in Second Life!

Choose one of the many different styles we have created for you. And remember, there are almost unlimited choices of how you can look after you enter Second Life!

These are just a few examples of what you can choose to get you started. You'll have plenty of opportunities to be almost anyone you want should you change your mind later.

(Skip this step)

CITY CHIC - MALE

(Choose this avatar)

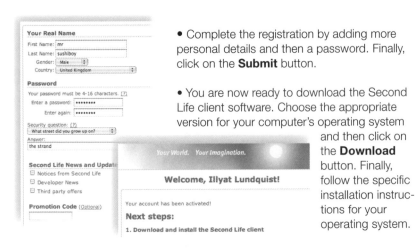

• Complete the registration by adding more personal details and then a password. Finally, click on the **Submit** button.

• You are now ready to download the Second Life client software. Choose the appropriate version for your computer's operating system and then click on the **Download** button. Finally, follow the specific installation instructions for your operating system.

Running Second Life

To join up to the Second Life network, launch the client program on your computer. Enter your registered **First Name**, **Last Name**, and **Password** and click on the **Connect** button. Now wait to be hooked up—this can take a few minutes the first time you try.

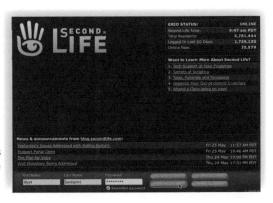

Shopping in Second Life

Second Life is a world where there are limitless possibilities for changing personal appearance, so if you stick to the basic defaults, you'll quickly be identified as "tourist." A few moments spent playing with the **Appearance** tools in the **Edit** menu will enable you to alter your look drastically—you can pretty well stretch or squash anything from your shirt to your head!

Of course, Second Life also features numerous stores where you can go to buy new clothes—and even the odd new body part. **Midnight City**, for example, is one of the oldest shopping centers in Second Life and is strewn with boutiques featuring creations from top designers, all of which can be procured by handing over your Linden dollars. Similarly, if you care to head off for the Lusk area you'll come across **Luskwood Creatures**—here you can get yourself some cool animal outfits, such as bats, skunk, foxes, wolves, or dragons. **Armord Tower** is the place to go if you want to fix up your avatar with robotic outifts and jetpacks. And at **Tableau** you can find some tasteful men's clothing.

You're now a part of a new virtual world! Your avatar will appear in the center of your screen with your name above your head. To begin with, all new members must attend Orientation Island. Here you will learn the basics of Second Life.

• To fly, click on the button at the foot of the screen marked **Fly,** and maneuver using the arrow keys on your keyboard. You can fly up or down using the **E** or **C** keys (or the **Page Up/Page Down** keys if you have them).

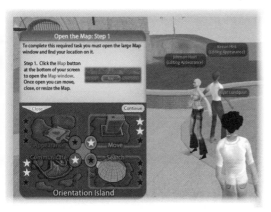

• To chat with another Lifer, go up to them, click on the **Chat** button, type in your text, and press the **Enter** key. Everyone in the close vicinity will be able to "hear" what you've said—the text will appear on their screen. If you want to talk with someone privately, then you can use the instant messenging facility—click on the **IM** button.

Pikipimp

http://www.pikipimp.com

Not exactly a game, but it is extremely good fun. Pikipimp allows you to upload a photograph and "pimp" your image by dragging and dropping items from the menu. For example, if you wish to add a mustache tp your picture, select Mustaches from the drop-down menu and choose one of the options and drag it into place. It's as simple as that. Other possibilities include adding funny hats, hair, lips, noses, and scars.

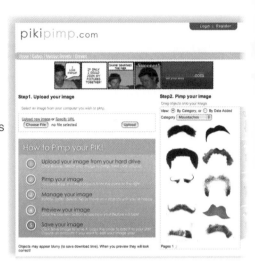

Arcaplay

http://www.arcaplay.com

Arcaplay is another well-sourced games directory. In particular, it benefits from its games being located in a series of well-organized categories. Many of the games within were produced using AJAX technologies. Unsurprisingly, given its name, Arcaplay is particularly stong on arcade-style games. Highlights include Fleabag

Vs Mutt, a "shoot-em-up" cat and dog caper, and Spooky Hoops, a basketball game where the player has to score without being caught by a skeleton.

Fleabag Vs Mutt

Spooky Hoops

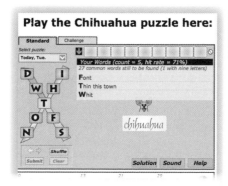

Chihuahua

http://chi.lexigame.com

Chihuahua is a Boggle-style game in which the object is to create as many possible words of four letters or more from a nine-letter selection. Click on the letters to make up the words. Players can match themselves against others in real time.

Sink My Ship

http://www.sinkmyship.com

Another online interactive version of a classic boardgame, Sink My Ship is a nice take on Battleship. The interface is slick, with excellent sound effects and some nice animated touches—for example, the crew of sunken vessels floating on the water in life boats. To set up, drag your boats onto the grid; to fire missiles, click on your enemy's cells.

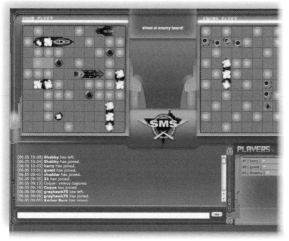

More Games Sites

Atomic Puzzle	http://www.king.com	Phrasr	http://www.pimpampum.net/phrasr
Auditorium	http://www.playauditorium.com	Play Portal	http://portal.wecreatestuff.com
Bloodwars	http://bloodwars.net	Quantum Legacy	http://quantumlegacy.com
Bubble Tanks	http://armorgames.com	Red Remover	http://www.thegamehomepage.com
Bunny Hunt	http://www.themaninblue.com	Runescape	http://www.runescape.com
Desktop Defender	http://www.kixeye.com	Sherwood Dungeon	http://www.sherwooddungeon.com
Fastr	http://randomchaos.com/games	Tag Man	http://www.apogee-web-consulting.com/tagman
		Zelderex	http://zelderex.com/

Kids' Sites

Although there has been plenty of adverse publicity about the use of the Internet by children, with common sense, care, and parental supervision the web can be an absolute treasure of education and entertainment. For the next four pages, I'll hand you over to someone with far greater experience in this field than I have—my eight-year-old son, Louis.

ICT Games

http://www.ictgames.com

ICT Games is a website that has awesome games for kids and most of them are educational too. So during computer class at school your child has an excuse: "But Miss, all I was doing was learning!"

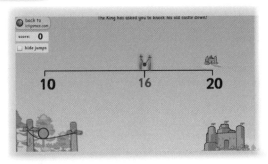

Panfu

http://www.panfu.com

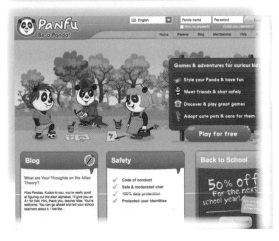

Panfu is a safe virtual world for children. You can style your panda and have fun. Meet friends and chat safely, and much more. Now you now don't have to worry about your kid chatting with people over the Internet.

(Interjection from Dad: *I still keep an eye on what you're doing, don't you worry!*)

SecretBuilders

http://www.secretbuilders.com/dw_new.html

SecretBuilders is another virtual world for kids. Unlike Panfu, you are a person in this world, not a panda. If you know Dizzywood, this is made by the same people.

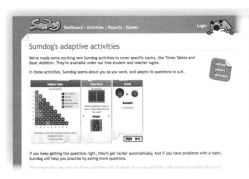

SumDog

http://www.sumdog.com

Sumdog is a website that has free math games. You can use it at school, at home, or just for general fun. It's great for adults, kids, and anyone else.

Play Kids Games

http://www.playkidsgames.com

This is a great educational gaming website for kids. There are math, alphabet, and memory games, and lots more. This website is also great for teaching.

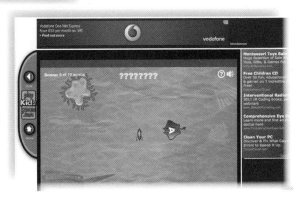

Yahoo! Kids

http://kids.yahoo.com

Yahoo! Kids is a very cool site. It has jokes, games, and a whole lot more. Sometimes there's even a sneak preview of a new TV show or movie. You can send e-cards, and there's also a study zone. Yes, it really deserves to be in this book!

National Geographic Kids

http://kids.nationalgeographic.com/kids

National Geographic Kids is a cool site where you can find out news and information about animals, and watch videos about nature. There are also lots of different games relating to animals.

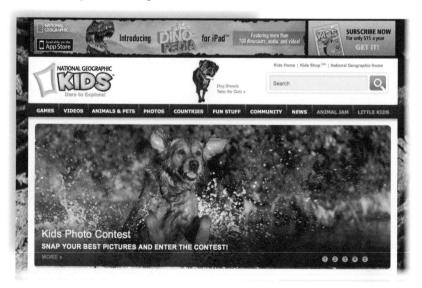

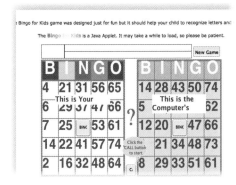

Bingo For Kids

http://www.allaboutstuff.
com/Kids_Games/Bingo_
for_Kids.asp

Most Bingo sites are for
adults, but this one is
designed for kids to play
against the computer.

A Small Car

http://www.freeonlinegames.com/game/a-small-car.html

A Small Car is a
simple game. You
have to drive around
a curvy road in a
little green car, but
it's VERY hard to
control. I know from
experience! There are
also hundreds of other
games on this site.

Children on the Internet

The sites listed below all provide detailed advice regarding online safety. They
are especially useful if you're concerned with the online activities of children or
teenagers.

Internet Crime Complaint Center	http://www.ic3.gov
NetSmartz	http://www.netsmartz.org
SafeFamilies	http://www.safefamilies.org
SafeTeens	http://www.safeteens.com
WebWiseKids	http://www.webwisekids.org

Mapping

In 1962, in his book *The Gutenberg Galaxy: The Making of Typographic Man*, Marshall McLuhan described how electronic mass media had turned the world into a "global village." While he was by no means the originator of the phrase, his prophetic use of the term has been used by successive generations as a metaphor to describe the impact of new technology on the way we live and communicate—since the early 1990s, this has generally referred to developments on the Internet.

Few aspects of the Web are more awe-inspiring than its ability to reduce the globe to the size of a computer screen. Anyone who has downloaded the satellite software Google Earth **(http://www.earth.google.com)** could surely never fail to be amazed at how it's possible to shrink an image of the planet taken in space to a single street with a few clicks of a mouse button. Indeed, if you live in a large city in the United States or Western Europe, you are more than likely to be able to see an aerial photograph of your home using this program. This section of the book will focus on how to use web-based maps.

Google Maps

http://maps.google.com

With its finger seemingly in all major web-related pies, here Google has provided a comprehensive mapping system that can be navigated by mouse to different levels of detail. Users may enter an area name, specific address, zip code (or its equivalent), or name a prominent location to quickly find it on the map. Google Maps also provides driving instructions between two locations, providing both a mapped diagram and a step-by-step list of how to get to a destination, along with estimates of how long the journey is likely to take. The system uses the same sources as Google Earth to provide high-resolution satellite images of most urban areas in the United States and Canada, and many others across the globe, including most of Europe and parts of South America, Australia, and the Far East.

Getting Started with Google Maps

Let's now take a look at Google Maps at work. We'll start off with a simple example of finding a location—in this case, 10 Downing Street, London—the residence of the British prime minister. Enter the URL: **http://maps.google.com**.

Google Maps launches with an overview map of the United States. The panel on the left enables the user to save their own maps or routes. The top left-hand corner of the map window shows a series of navigation controls. You can click on any of the buttons to maneuver around the map (*see box on right*). If you have a mouse with a scroll wheel, you may be able to use that to zoom in and out.

Entering Map Locations

To find a map location, type it into the box near the top of the screen. Google Maps can interpret country, city, and street names, as well as zip codes and their international equivalents. In this case, we have entered **London SW1A 2AA** (the post code of 10 Downing Street). Click on the **Search** button.

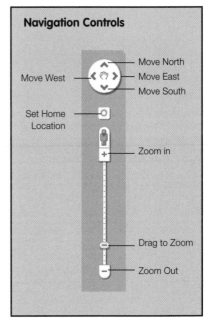

• You will now see a detailed map of the London address you chose (*see above*). This shows the map zoomed in to the maximum level of detail.

• A pop-up balloon will appear that contains the details of the address. It is linked to a marker on the map. You can store this location in your own **My Maps** list—it will remain in place on your map each time you open it up. Click on the button marked **Save in My Maps**.

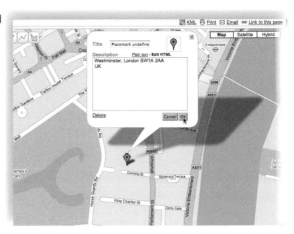

• Give your location a title, and click on the **OK** button.

• Your My Maps list will open on the left-hand side of the screen. There you'll see the location that you have just entered. Click on the **Save** button to store your information.

Finding a Route Between Two Locations

Google Maps will also provide you with optimum routes between two different points. Let's now try to discover the quickest way to get between 10 Downing Street and the British Museum. (For this example we've already set up the latter location.)

• Click on the **Downing Street** marker. Then in the pop-up balloon click on the text labeled **From Here**.

• A new pop-up balloon appears. Enter your destination in the box marked **End Address**. Click on the **Go** button.

• The route between the two destinations is shown on the map. To the left of the map, there is a list of road directions, distances, and times involved in the journey.

Alternative Views

Google Maps allows you to see a marked road-style map, a satellite photograph, or a hybrid of the two. Let's see how these work.

• In the top right-hand corner, click on the button marked **Satellite**.

• Your map has now transformed into a satellite photograph of the same area. These are the same images found when using the Google Earth software.

• Return to the top right-hand corner of the screen and click on the button marked **Hybrid**.

• The street names from the map are now applied to the satellite photograph. (Throughout these changes, the route line between destinations remains visible.)

Close Zoom

We'll now take a look at the highest available photographic resolution of our chosen destination.

• Click on the **Satellite** button. This will remove the street names from your map. In the **Navigation Control**, click on the button marked "**+**" until the photograph reaches its maximum level of magnification.

• This is a satellite aerial view of Number 10 Downing Street, London. As you can see, your location marker remains in place (*see bottom left of the picture*). Such high-resolution images are not available everywhere but will be possible for most major cities.

Out of This World

Google Maps are not restricted to our own planet. There are NASA maps of some parts of the moon available (**http://moon.google .com**) as well as an infrared map of the surface of Mars (**http://www.google .com/mars**). *(See right.)* The moon maps contain location markers for all of NASA's previous moon landings.

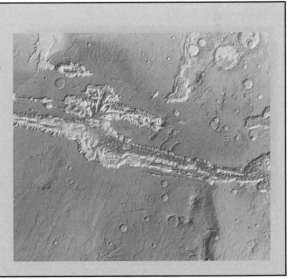

What's Nearby?

When you store locations on your Google Map, you have the option of making them public or private. If they are public, then others may find them in searches. Let's take a look at some potential uses for this idea.

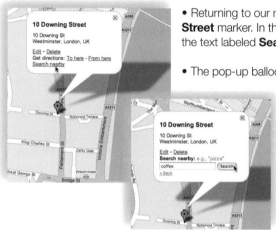

• Returning to our map, click on the **Downing Street** marker. In the pop-up balloon, click on the text labeled **Search Nearby**.

• The pop-up balloon will expand to include a search box. In this example we'll try to find a coffee bar as close as possible to 10 Downing Street. Type **Coffee** in the box and click on the **Search** button.

The map will now show any nearby markers that have been tagged "coffee." The markers are labeled from A to Z, reflecting how close they are to the chosen location. There is a key to this list down the left-hand side of the screen. You can click on any of these markers to find more information.

Google Maps Controversies

As astonishing as the technology behind Google Maps may be, there have been numerous fears raised on issues of privacy, especially regarding the detail of Street View (*see right*) that can render individual faces recognizable. This has also created some accidentally humorous moments, as hapless individuals have been caught on camera engaging in activities they presumably would not have wanted presented to the world.

Google Street View

Introduced in 2007, Street View takes Google Maps a step further by photographing the world at street level and making it possible to navigate via the web browser. Street View has been captured in many large cities and towns throughout Europe and America. Let's take an example, looking at a Street View map for the Colosseum, in Rome.

• Begin by typing **Colosseum, Rome** in the search box. The famous building is easily identifed on the map. Above the navigation bar, look for the "human" symbol—the little stick person—and drag the icon into the middle of the map, dropping it in the center of the Coloseum.

• You will now see an image from inside of the Colosseum. You can now drag the image around the screen and enjoy the 360-degree vista.

Planiglobe

http://www.planiglobe.com

A different—and simpler—approach comes from Planiglobe. This website enables users to create digital maps for download in EPS or vector form—

which can be imported by such graphics programs as Adobe Illustrator. They can then be used in any digital documents.

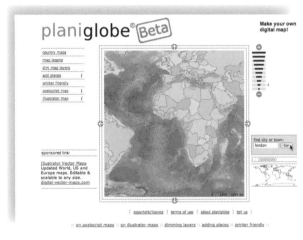

• Enter the URL: **http://www. planiglobe.com**.

• In the box labeled **Find City or Town**, type in your chosen location name—in this example, we'll use **London**.

• If your search yields more than one result, a pop-up window will emerge listing all of the available possibilities. Choose one from the list and click on the arrow button.

• To create your digital map, click on either the **Postscript Map** or **Illustrator Map** buttons, depending on the format you require. The digital files will then be downloaded to your hard drive.

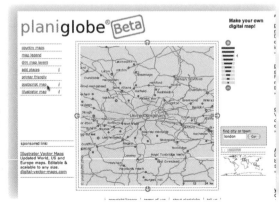

Tagzania

http://www.tagzania.com

Tagzania is a cross between tagging and mapping. Users may mark any locations they choose and allocate multiple tags to them. If you perform a keyword text search, you'll see a standard Google map with the Tagzania markers in position.

Wayfaring

http://www.wayfaring.com

This site crosses Google Maps with social networking. Users can set up their own maps, make them public, and other users can comment on them. The map at the foot of the page features one user's guide to his favorite restaurants in Seattle.

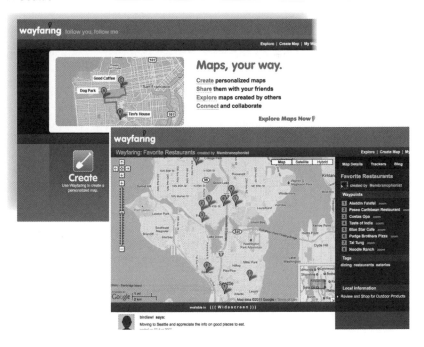

Music

Easy-to-access music content was one of the factors that drove the great demand for faster Internet connection speeds. This in turn fueled music download culture as a whole, creating a generation of potential consumers who rarely went anywhere near a music store to buy a CD. Much of the well-documented illegal activity takes place on news groups or peer-to-peer file sharing networks. Here, however, we'll look at legitimate ways to listen to music on the Internet—in particular, some that have successfully integrated aspects of social networking.

Last.fm

http://www.last.fm

Last.fm is a UK-based Internet radio station and music community website. It was founded in 2002 and is one of the world's largest social music platforms, with an estimated active user base of over 15 million listeners in more than 232 countries. Last.fm evolved out of the merger of two different applications: Audioscrobbler was a music recommendation system that began as a computer science project by Richard Jones, an undergraduate at the University of Southampton in the UK. Last.fm was founded in Germany as an Internet radio station and music community website but used similar music profiles to generate playlists, with "love" and "ban" buttons enabling users to customize their profiles. In 2003 the Audioscrobbler and Last.fm teams merged and set up headquarters in London. In summer 2007, the company was acquired by CBS Interactive for $280 million, but its creators remained at the helm.

Last.fm in Use

At the heart of Last.fm remains the "Audioscrobbler" music recommendation system, which enables the creation of a detailed profile of each user's musical tastes based on storing details of all the songs the user plays, either on the streamed radio station or on the user's own computer or mp3 player. This data is then "scrobbled"— transferred to the Last.fm database—via a plug-in. Profile data can be viewed on the user's personal webpage. Registration is necessary to set up a profile but is not necessary to view the Last.fm website or listen to radio stations. With over 10 million tracks "scrobbled" each day, the popularity of the site at peak times can cause the databases to overload. Last.fm also offers numerous social networking features. For example, it can recommend and play artists similar to the user's favorites.

Let's now look at some examples of Last.fm in action. Here we'll select a band, see what's available by them, and then see if it can recommend any music in a similar style.

• Begin by entering the URL: **http://www.last.fm**. If you are already registered then log in—click on Login and follow the instructions.

• On the following page, enter the name of the musician or band you wish to seek in the **Music Search** box on the top right-hand corner of the screen.

In this case we'll look up the Japanese rock band **Boris**. As you type in each letter, suggestions will appear in a drop-down menu. In this case, Boris appears in the list, so you can click on the name.

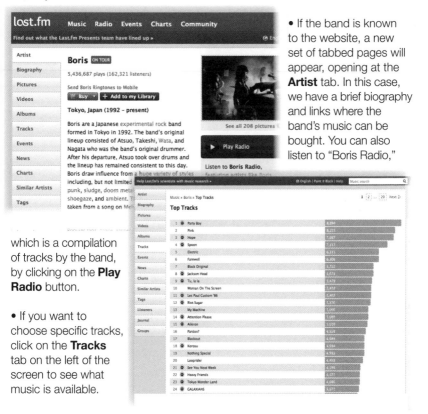

• If the band is known to the website, a new set of tabbed pages will appear, opening at the **Artist** tab. In this case, we have a brief biography and links where the band's music can be bought. You can also listen to "Boris Radio,"

which is a compilation of tracks by the band, by clicking on the **Play Radio** button.

• If you want to choose specific tracks, click on the **Tracks** tab on the left of the screen to see what music is available.

More Tabs

Let's take a brief look at more of the tabs on the left of the screen. As you can see, you can watch videos by the band, or look at photographs, discographies, biographies, and even latest events in which the band is involved. Significantly, much of this information is provided by Last.fm users. For example, the biography page (click on the **Bio** button) takes the form of a "wiki" and can be written and edited by any registered users. Below you can see the **Pictures**, **Events**, and **Biography** pages.

• Now let's look at some of the suggestions that Last.fm can identify. If you click on the **Tags** tab, you will see a "cloud" of categories created by other users and applied to Boris. In this case, let's click on the tag marked **Doom Metal**.

• You'll now see a specific Doom Metal page, with links to other bands that have also been tagged in the same way.

Pandora

http://www.pandora.com

Not dissimilar to Last.fm, Pandora is an automated recommendation and Internet radio service created by the Music Genome Project. Users enter a song or artist, and the service responds by playing selections that it believes to be musically similar. Users can then provide feedback on the accuracy of song choices—the system then takes that into account for future selections.

Over 400 different musical attributes (or "genes") are taken into account when suggesting tracks. If we look at a selection beginning with the letter "H," we find: "hand percussion," "hard bop qualities," "hard bop roots," "hard rock roots," "hardcore rap attitude," and "harmonica playing." These 400 attributes are combined into larger groups called "focus traits," of which there are 2,000.

So let's see Pandora in action. (Pandora is only available for use in North America.)

• Begin by entering Pandora's URL: **http://www.pandora.com**. Type in the name of the artist or song that interests you, and Pandora will create a personal streamed radio station based on your request. In this example, we've entered **The Stooges**. Click on the button marked **Listen Now**.

• Pandora will select your first track. If you like the track, you can click on the **Thumbs-Up** button; if you don't, click on the **Thumbs-Down** button.

To find out more information about the track, or where to buy it, click on the **Arrow** button in between the thumb buttons. If you want to move past the track, click on the **Fast-Forward** button, on the right of the navigation bar, and Pandora will begin to play the second selection it has come up with for you.

Yahoo! Music

http://new.music.yahoo.com

One of the most popular Internet sites of its kind, Yahoo! Music provides a variety of music services, including Internet radio, music videos, news, artist information, and original programming.

It began life as a magazine called *Launch*, which was issued in both standard print format and as an interactive CD-ROM. The service was purchased by Yahoo! in 2001 for $12 million and integrated into its website. Unlike Last.fm, which has a large core of "underground" music fans, Yahoo! Music is resolutely mainstream.

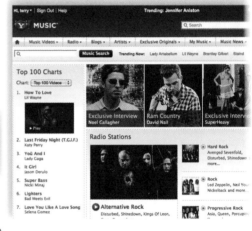

eJamming

http://www.ejamming.com

An interesting experiment with huge possibilities for musicians, eJamming has been touted as a kind of Skype for musicians. This is not a web-based product but downloadable peer-to-peer software that enables musicians to play with one another remotely. The cofounder, Alan Glueckman, conceived eJamming with his his cousin in mind—Aerosmith's drummer Joey Kramer—so that the band could still rehearse when one or more of its members were away. It's not, in fact, known if Aerosmith has tried it out, though.

The technology requires very high quality audio, and there has to be very low audio latency—the microsecond delays that can affect timing when recording and playing music using computers.

There's also a social networking angle to eJamming in that it aims to put like-minded musicians together. However, it isn't a free service—at $15 per month per person, that can mount up over an entire band.

Kompoz

http://www.kompoz.com

A slightly different approach to eJamming, Kompoz is aimed at collaborative composition and recording rather than live performance. A musician will kick off a new project by uploading an audio file and other musicians can then add their own parts. As new files are added, previous files are given a version number, so there's a record of the history and progress of the work. Each new project has its own workspace, which includes a forum where ideas, lyrics, chord charts, and the like can be discussed.

The H-Lounge

http://www.h-lounge.com

H-Lounge is a well-established digital music distributor that enables artists, musicians, and labels to sell their music directly to the public as mp3s, ringtones, or Skypetones.

Napster

http://www.napster.com

Once the scourge of the global music industry, Napster began life in 1999 as a peer-to-peer system and quickly established itself as *the* most significant source of illegal music sharing. After some heavy duty litigation, Napster abandoned the peer-to-peer software and set itself up as a legal music streaming system. It claims to have more the 15 million tracks that registered users can access for a monthly subscription.

Spotify

http://www.spotify.com

Probably the the most widely used music-streaming service, Spotify was launched in Sweden in 2008. Three years later Spotify could boast over 10 million users, over a million of whom were monthly subscribers. The user downloads client software, which then connects to the Internet. Music can be browsed by artist, album, record label, genre, or playlist as well as by keyword searches. For much of the music on Spotify, links enable the listener to buy downloads via partner retailers.

There are two kinds of account available. The free version is paid for by old-style radio ads, which cut in between tracks; Premium subscribers can avoid the ads and are also offered a range of extra features, such as higher quality streams, offline access, or use of Spotify on smartphones or other mobile devices.

Using Spotify

Begin by entering the URL: **http://www.spotify.com**. Click on the **Download Spotify** button. When that's completed, follow the installation instructions for your chosen operating system.

• Register for Spotify and then log in with your user ID and password.

• The main Spotify window contains a search box at the top, and the ability to create your own playlists.

• To play a song, click on the track name in the main window and then on the **Play** button at the bottom of the screen.

• The **Get** button indicates that the track can be purchased for download.

• You can also link your Spotify listening to your Facebook page by clicking on the **Connect to Facebook** button.

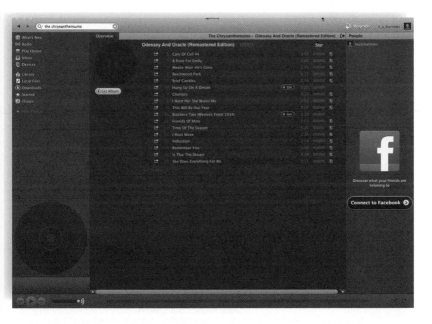

More Music Sites

Dottunes	http://www.dottunes.net	SideLoad	http://www.sideload.com
Jamendo	http://www.jamendo.com	Snaptune	http://www.snaptune.com
Musipedia	http://www.musipedia.org	Streampad	http://www.streampad.com
PodBop	http://podbop.org	Tubes	http://www.tubesmusic.com
RateYourMusic	http://rateyourmusic.com	UpTo11	http://upto11.net

News

Some of the most successful websites of the past decade—at least in terms of regular and loyal users—have been news broadcast sites. The BBC "ticker" website, for example, is one of the most popular news sites in the world. Also widely viewed are sites allied to the most popular daily broadsheet newspapers. Some of these sites, while not necessarily at the technical sharp end, paved the way for innovations in website technology, such as RSS newsfeeds, podcasts, and allowing readers the opportunity to make comments on some of their news stories. The most innovative of the current crop of news websites are those that draw their stories from a wide variety of other sites, or those whose users have acted as editors in selecting stories.

Bits of News

http://www.bitsofnews.com

A vast scrolling news resource, Bits of News contains items from across the world on a wide range of topics, including politics, culture, economics, science, and technology. Registered users are able to submit news stories they have found elsewhere to the site's editorial staff.

A particularly valuable aspect of the Bits of News site can be found in the sidebars, which contains links to most of the major British and American news sources on the Internet. Stories can also be syndicated via RSS, ATOM, and Delicious and other distribution methods.

Clipmarks

http://www.clipmarks.com

As with many aspects of this book, there is considerable crossover between some of the sections: Clipmarks could equally be termed a social bookmarking site or a blogging tool. It was founded by New York lawyer Eric Goldstein, who claims to have been inspired by cutting and pasting from the Web into a Word file only to create an unreadable mess. It is an application that enables users to clip and save information from the Web. This need not be an entire website or news story, but simply the interesting part. Clips can be stored privately, tagged

and made public, or attached to blogs. Clipmarks uses a browser plug-in that brings up an interactive clipping menu. When you scroll over text, Clipmarks highlights it and allows you to clip it and store it on the Clipmarks server.

Newsvine

http://www.newsvine.com

Based in Seattle, Washington, Newsvine is a website consisting of community-driven news stories and opinions. Users can write articles and save links to external content, vote, comment, and chat on article pages created both by users and by journalists from the Associated Press, ESPN, and New Scientist.

Wired

http://www.wired.com

One of the
Internet's best-
loved magazines,
the Wired website
is a rich source of
news stories on
technology, science,
culture, business,
and politics.
Indeed, if you're
at all interested in
the cutting edge of
technology, Wired is
a must-read journal.

Topix

http://www.topix.com

Topix is a discussion board website
specializing in bringing together news
stories for a specific area. It began
life in 2002 as a news aggregator,
categorizing news stories by topic
and geography. The company migrated
to the topix.com domain in 2007, and
invited the involvement of over
100 journalists and editors from
well-known newspapers, as well as
volunteers from the public.

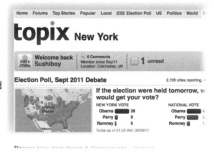

Topix in Use

Let's look at how effective Topix can be in practice. Begin by entering the URL—
http://www.topix.com.

• Click on the **Change City** button.

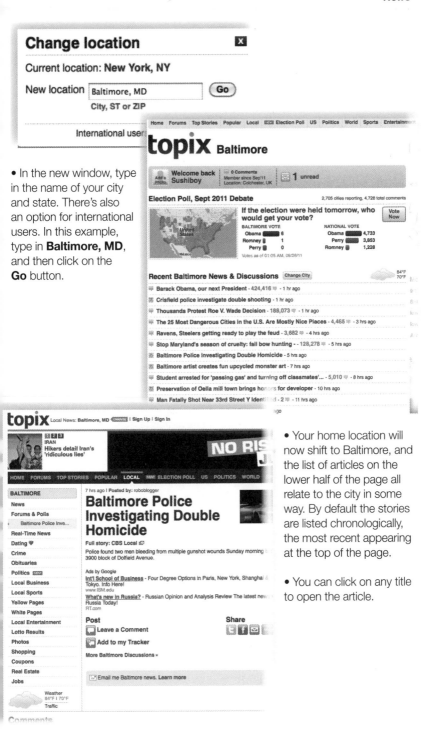

Change location ☒

Current location: **New York, NY**

New location [Baltimore, MD] (Go)
City, ST or ZIP

International user

• In the new window, type in the name of your city and state. There's also an option for international users. In this example, type in **Baltimore, MD**, and then click on the **Go** button.

Home Forums Top Stories Popular Local NEW Election Poll US Politics World Sports Entertainment

topix Baltimore

Welcome back 0 Comments ☒ 1 unread
Add a Photo Sushiboy Member since Sep'11
Location: Colchester, UK

Election Poll, Sept 2011 Debate 2,705 cities reporting, 4,728 total comments

If the election were held tomorrow, who would get your vote? [Vote Now]
BALTIMORE VOTE   NATIONAL VOTE
Obama ▇▇▇ 6   Obama ▇▇▇ 4,733
Romney ▇ 1   Perry ▇▇ 3,853
Perry ▇ 0   Romney ▇ 1,228
Votes as of 01:05 AM, 09/26/11

Recent Baltimore News & Discussions [Change City]   84°F 70°F

▪ Barack Obama, our next President - 424,416 ⚐ - 1 hr ago
▪ Crisfield police investigate double shooting - 1 hr ago
▪ Thousands Protest Roe V. Wade Decision - 188,073 ⚐ - 1 hr ago
▪ The 25 Most Dangerous Cities in the U.S. Are Mostly Nice Places - 4,465 ⚐ - 3 hrs ago
▪ Ravens, Steelers getting ready to play the feud - 3,682 ⚐ - 4 hrs ago
▪ Stop Maryland's season of cruelty: fall bow hunting - - 128,278 ⚐ - 5 hrs ago
▪ Baltimore Police investigating Double Homicide - 5 hrs ago
▪ Baltimore artist creates fun upcycled monster art - 7 hrs ago
▪ Student arrested for 'passing gas' and turning off classmates'... - 5,010 ⚐ - 8 hrs ago
▪ Preservation of Oella mill town brings honors for developer - 10 hrs ago
▪ Man Fatally Shot Near 33rd Street Y Identified - 2 ⚐ - 11 hrs ago

topix Local News: Baltimore, MD CHANGE | Sign Up | Sign In

IRAN
Hikers detail Iran's 'ridiculous lies'

NO RIS

HOME FORUMS TOP STORIES POPULAR LOCAL NEW ELECTION POLL US POLITICS WORLD

BALTIMORE
News
Forums & Polls
  Baltimore Police Inve...
Real-Time News
Dating ♥
Crime
Obituaries
Politics NEW
Local Business
Local Sports
Yellow Pages
White Pages
Local Entertainment
Lotto Results
Photos
Shopping
Coupons
Real Estate
Jobs
  Weather 84°F | 70°F
  Traffic

7 hrs ago | Posted by: robotblogger

Baltimore Police Investigating Double Homicide

Full story: CBS Local ☒

Police found two men bleeding from multiple gunshot wounds Sunday morning 3900 block of Dolfield Avenue.

Ads by Google
Int'l School of Business - Four Degree Options in Paris, New York, Shanghai & Tokyo. Info Here!
www.ISM.edu
What's new in Russia? - Russian Opinion and Analysis Review The latest new Russia Today!
RT.com

Post   Share
📝 Leave a Comment   🇹 🇫 ✉ ▪
📷 Add to my Tracker
More Baltimore Discussions »

✉ Email me Baltimore news. Learn more

• Your home location will now shift to Baltimore, and the list of articles on the lower half of the page all relate to the city in some way. By default the stories are listed chronologically, the most recent appearing at the top of the page.

• You can click on any title to open the article.

Comments

BBC News

http://www.bbc.co.uk/news

Launched in 1997, BBC News Online is Europe's most popular news website, drawing in over 14 million unique viewers each week. Coverage is international with a focus on Britain and the United States. It also features an in-depth sports website. Starting in 2008, each article index was given its own RSS 2.0 feed, making it easy to subscribe to areas of particular interest.

The Washington Post

http://www.washingtonpost.com

One of America's most notable broadsheet newspapers, the *Washington Post*'s online edition is also well known for its interesting selection of podcasts.

Reuters

http://www.reuters.com

Founded in 1851 by Paul Julius Reuter, who realized that with the emerging telegraph technology it would no longer take several days to source international stories, Reuters has established itself as one of the world's leading news agencies.

Yahoo! News

http://news.yahoo.com

One of America's most popular sites of its type, Yahoo! News is an online news aggregator featuring international news stories, weighted toward US interest. Articles are drawn primarily from news services such as Associated Press, Reuters, Agence France-Presse, Fox News, Christian Science Monitor, USA Today, CNN, CBC News, and the BBC. Users are allowed to comment on many news stories.

USA Today

http://www.usatoday.com

One of one America's highest circulation newspapers, the online version of *USA Today* shares the newspaper's easy-to-read style, as well as its fondness for infographics and color-coded sections.

Peer-to-Peer Sharing

One of the most controversial aspects of the Internet over the past decade, peer-to-peer (or "P2P" as it's usually known) is a method of sharing files between two computers. It has been the bane of the world's media industries since it came to prominence in the late 1990s, when increasing numbers of young people started using programs such as Napster to illegally download mp3s of music, causing CDs sales to fall sharply. In turn, this aided the acceptance of the mp3 format, the appeal of which was that it could produce an audio quality not vastly lower than a CD, but at less than a tenth of the size—making download times substantially faster. More recently, BitTorrents have taken P2P file sharing further, enabling much larger files, such as video formats or computer software, to be distributed across the Internet.

theguardian

News | Sport | Comment | Culture | Business | Money | Life & style

Business 〉 Music industry 〉

Global recorded music sales fall almost $1.5bn amid increased piracy
UK loses mantle as third-largest music market after 'physical' sales of CDs collapse by almost a fifth

Mark Sweney
guardian.co.uk, Monday 28 March 2011 15.38 BST
Article history

A Brief History of File Sharing

In the early days of the Internet, the only effective way of sharing large files was by FTP (File Transfer Protocol). An anonymous FTP server would allow users to send or receive files to or from one another. It was a messy process, very user *un*friendly, and was only understood by those with technical savvy. However, for most people, the principal impediment was more basic—the slow speed of domestic Internet connections. Large music and video files could take hours (even days!) to download.

In 1999, Napster made its mark on the world as the first popular P2P application, taking advantage of the development of file compression techniques that would give birth to the mp3 format. At its peak in 2001, it was estimated that there were 60 million Napster users across the globe—and that was beginning to bite significantly into the world's commercial CD markets. Unsurprisingly, the major music labels began to flex their muscles, threatening both the P2P software providers and music downloaders with legal action. However, the main problem they faced was that there was nothing intrinsically wrong in allowing people to copy legal files from one computer to another. And how would Napster and other networks be able to tell what was legal and what was not? Furthermore, so many people were now engaged in illegal music copying that it was simply not practical to launch lawsuits against individuals. In the end, Napster in its original form was

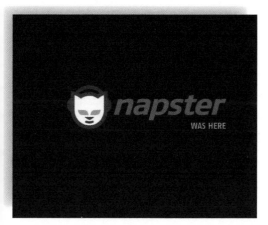

put out of business by the sheer bulk of filed lawsuits and attempts at reaching out-of-court settlements. The same fate befell WinMX, the other major P2P application of the early 1990s. However, as soon as one P2P ceased operation, others emerged to fill the hole, and it was clear that chasing downloaders, uploaders, and software developers through the courts was not a long-term solution. Some turned toward other tactics, such

as making legal downloads more attractive. But, in truth, the mass acceptance of download culture has forced the industry to reconsider what it considers to be commercial "product"—and recorded music is accepted as no longer being the earner it once was.

P2P applications, whether of the traditional variety or the more recent BitTorrent style, continue to increase in popularity.

How Does P2P Work?

The basic concept of P2P is pretty simple: a person with a fast Internet connection runs a dedicated piece of software that links their computer to a network of other users who are hooked up to the same network at that moment in time. Users will make a selection of files on their hard drives available for sharing. Anyone looking for a specific item will use a search feature built into the software to see if it matches anything offered within the network. If they see something they like, they can then download that file directly from the other person's computer. There are a large number of different popular P2P programs—Kazaa, imesh, SoulSeek, and BearShare, for example. All of these can be downloaded free of charge.

More recently, a different approach to P2P has taken over in popularity. BitTorrents work by downloading small segments of files from many different websites at the same time. This takes the pressure away from the file sharer, who only has to upload once. This is especially significant for those with monthly bandwidth allowances set by their ISPs, which can easily be eroded if a large number of individuals decide they want to download their files.

BitTorrents are widely used for sharing video material—indeed there have been cases of feature films being pirated and made available in this way before their official release. Not that we are endorsing such practices in this book, of course.

SoulSeek

http://www.slsknet.org

If you are interested in music—especially of the independent variety—then SoulSeek is the place you need to start out. The work of former Napster programmer Nir Arbel, SoulSeek relies on its own central server. It has one major advantage over most other traditional P2P programs in that it has the capability of selecting and downloading a complete folder of files. This saves time if you want to download a complete album's worth of mp3s—to do the same with other P2P software you would have to figure out which tracks made up the album, and then select and download each file independently.

SoulSeek is popular with producers and musicians, so there is a good deal of music available legitimately. And, of course, a great deal that is not.

Using SoulSeek

To download software for Windows computers, go to the SoulSeek website, which is **http://www.slsknet.org/download.html**. For Mac users, you can download a program called SoulseeX from **http://chris.schleifer.net**.

• Launch your chosen software.

• In the **Query** box at the top of the screen, type in your search text. Press the **Enter** key.

• The files available for download appear in staggered folders. The sharer has a top-level folder, which may contain a number of album folders, each of which contain mp3 files. You can download individual files, albums, or *everything* that user has on offer. (Note: SoulSeek users may prevent anyone they choose from downloading their files: taking too much while sharing too little is one of the most common reasons for such "bans" taking place.)

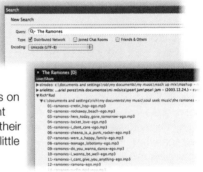

isoHunt

http://www.isohunt.org

Established in 2003, isoHunt is an extremely useful P2P and Torrent search engine directory with its own forum.

BitTorrent

http://www.bittorrent.com

Although BitTorrent is now the most popular mode of sharing software, music videos, and digital books, by Internet standards its take off was quite sluggish. The first torrent network was created in 2001 by a Python-language programmer named Bram Cohen. His intention was to share it freely. However, it wasn't until 2005 that the rest of the world caught on.

So how is BitTorrent different from previous P2P networks like Gnutella and Kazaa? As we've already said, the latter networks depend on the uploader repeatedly transferring files as requested. BitTorrent, on the other hand, is a true P2P network in that it is the user base as a whole that does the file serving.

How Does It Work?

Two key phrases to understand with torrent sharing are "swarming" and "tracking." Swarming refers to splitting large files into hundreds of smaller segments and then sharing them across a "swarm" of linked users. Downloading a large number of small segments from many different sources at the same time prevents the bottlenecking that occurs with single-source sharing and thus is much faster.

Tracking refers to specific servers that help members of the "swarm" find one another. Special torrent software—as we'll see on the next page—is used to upload, download, and reconstruct the segments into complete files; torrent text files act as pointers during this process.

The way torrents work actively encourages users to share (or "seed") their files while punishing users who "leech"—take files without sharing. Download speeds are controlled by BitTorrent tracking servers, who monitor the swarm. If you are identified as a seed, servers will reward you by increasing your bandwidth; if you are a leech, the tracking servers can choke your download speeds almost to a standstill. Leeches are unwelcome in a BitTorrent!

BitTorrent is by no means for the impatient, and it certainly does take a while (and a little technical know-how) to set up a computer for dealing with torrents. But the results can be very worthwhile, especially if it's your intention to share very large files.

How to Use Torrent Sharing

There are four different elements that you need (or need access to) to set yourself up for torrent sharing:

- BitTorrent client software for uploading, downloading, and constructing files
- Tracker server
- Torrent text file that points to the files you want to download
- Torrent search engine that helps you find torrent text files
- A high-speed Internet connection with an ISP that will allow torrent file trading

Now let's take a step-by-step walk through the complete torrent process. You may need some patience here—this is one area covered in this book that can be taxing from a technical point of view.

Client Software

Begin by downloading and installing your BitTorrent client software. (A list is shown at the foot of the page.) Initially, you don't need to launch the program, but it should be in place, ready for action.

Torrent Search Engine

Use a special torrent search engine to find torrent text files on the Internet. (A list is shown across the page.) In spite of what some business executives and other authorities would imply, using Person-To-Person technology is a *completely* legal activity. However, nobody is under any pretence that a great deal of what takes place in the P2P online world does infringe copyright law—and in some cases may go much further, as a source of illegal material that later finds itself used on pirated copies of DVDs and CDs. Periodically, therefore, you will find even some of the best-known torrent search engines have been closed down pending legal action: they usually pop back up again within a matter of days. It's a good idea to keep abreast of these activities, though. If you type "Torrent Search Engines" into Google from time to time, you should find up-to-date lists of currently active servers.

Now let's try a torrent search of our own. In this example we'll use the popular IsoHunt, and we'll continue our search for items related to the band The Ramones.

Torrent Software

Anatomic P2P	http://developer.berlios.de/projects/anatomic
BitComet	http://www.bitcomet.com
BitLord	http://www.bitlord.com
BitSpirit	http://www.167bt.com/intl
BitTornado	http://www.bittornado.com
BitTorrent	http://www.bittorrent.com
uTorrent	http://www.utorrent.com
Vuze	http://www.vuze.com

Torrent Search Engines

Demoniod	http://www.demonoid.com	TorrentScan	http://www.torrentscan.com
Fenopy	http://www.fenopy.com	TorrentSpy	http://www.torrentspy.com
LegalTorrents	http://www.legaltorrents.com	Yotoshi	http://www.yotoshi.com
MegaNova	http://www.meganova.org		
Mininova	http://www.mininova.org		
The Pirate Bay	http://www.piratebay.com		
Torrent	http://www.torrent-damage.net		
Torrentbox	http://www.torrentbox.com		
Torrentmatrix	http://www.torrentmatrix.com		
Torrentportal	http://www.torrentportal.com		
IsoHunt	http://www.isohunt.com		
TorrentReactor	http://www.torrentreactor.to		
Torrents	http://www.torrents.to		

• Enter the URL: **http:// www.isohunt.com**. Type your search criteria into the box at the top of the screen, and then click on the button marked **Loading**.

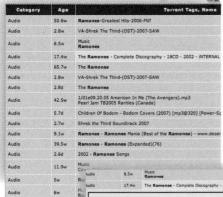

• As you can see, there are a number of matches. Click on one that interests you. The row will open out details of the trackers. Click on the button marked **Download .torrent**. The torrent text file will now download onto your hard drive.

Downloading

Now is the time to run your client program. In this example, we've downloaded and installed the current version of BitTorrent—the program designed by Bram Cohen (**http://www.bittorrent.com**).

• Locate the downloaded torrent file on your desktop. Launch the BitTorrent software. Drag the downloaded file and drop it in the main window of BitTorrent.

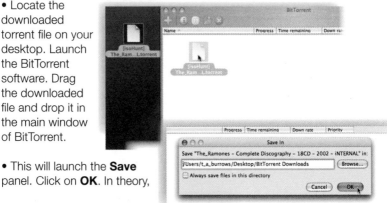

• This will launch the **Save** panel. Click on **OK**. In theory,

the download could now begin. However, before that happens, there will be a good deal of background interaction between your program and the tracker server while it scours the Internet for people with whom to swarm. This can take several minutes. Both the client and tracker server will specifically be looking for other users who have the same torrent text file as you. As the server discovers users to swarm with, each one will be labeled as a leech or a seed: the more seeds the tracker finds for you, the faster your download will be.

It's also good form in the file-sharing community to leave your torrent software running for a few hours after a download has completed, enabling you to share your reconstructed files with other users.

Uploading

Now we'll look briefly at the reverse of this process—uploading files to share. We'll use the BitTorrent client software once again.

• From the File menu, choose the option **Make New Torrent**.

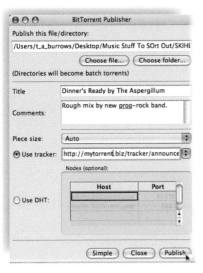

• The **Publishing** window will open. Enter the name of the file on your hard drive that you wish upload—you can type it in manually, or you can click on the **Browse File** button and navigate your hard drive until you find it.

• Add a title and comments for your file.

• You must now decide where to publish your tracker file. If you know the URL of a tracker site you intend to use, click on the **Use Tracker** button and enter it in the box alongside; if you don't have access to a public tracker you can use DHT—this essentially tells the BitTorrent software to act as its own tracker. This will be less effective than using a *real* tracker, though. (There are websites that contain lists of public tracker sites, such as **http://thebeehive.info**.)

• Click on the **Publish** button.

• BitTorrent will prepare your file. Click on the button marked **Start Seeding**. Your file is now being made available to other P2P users on the network.

Important Legal/Moral Note

Peer-to-peer networking is, in itself, a completely legal activity. However, downloading other people's copyrighted material using P2P is not, and unfortunately many people use it just for that purpose. In the future, this may well herald a completely new approach to the idea of intellectual property rights, or the way in which we receive our media content; or it may equally keep the legal profession in its accustomed style for decades to come. Whatever happens, we should stress firmly that this book (and this section in particular) is *in no way* intended to encourage copyright infringement. And that no illegal content has been downloaded in the making of this book. Honest! Our advice on this matter is simple: understand the law of your land, make your own moral judgements, and act accordingly.

Personal Management Tools

In this section we will be taking a look at web-based applications that are aimed at promoting greater personal efficiency. You'll see that some of these are perhaps more work-oriented, although they'll also come in useful for anyone leading a busy social life. In the not-so-distant past, the standard method of keeping your work and leisure time under control was to use a personal organizer system, such as those famously produced by Filofax or Time Manager International. These days, many of us are more likely to use computers for scheduling meetings and general project management. A new generation of web-based software takes this approach a stage further in that it enables groups of people to share such information. If, for example, you were to keep an up-to-date online diary, then others would automatically be able to see when you were available. If someone were trying to organize a meeting with a large group of people, the software itself could even come up with convenient dates and times because it would have access to the availability of everyone involved. Let's begin with a brief look at some of the free online calendar systems available.

30 Boxes

http://www.30boxes.com

Launched in 2006, 30 Boxes was created by a small San Francisco–based company called 83°. Using AJAX technology, 30 Boxes combines a calendar/diary system with assorted social networking functions. However, its most innovative and useful feature is its ability to integrate with many other applications, such as Facebook, Twitter, Flickr, Webshots, Upcoming, LiveJournal, WordPress, Vox, and MySpace.

Free Sign Up   email address   •••••••••

30 Boxes™ lets you connect with people who matter **most**.

▢ Remember Birthdays
▢ Know What's Going On
▢ Get Stuff Done
▢ Keep Up With Friends
▢ Painless Organization / Sharing

👤 Hi, I'm Julie from 30B.
You're invited to try the world's best online calendar.

or just get started!

© 2007 83° | Other good stuff. Our Blog, Buddy Cards, 30 Boxed, Blog Timeline, Peopl

In truth, this is such an in-depth application that we can only scratch the surface in a few pages, but it really is worth investigating in more detail. As the *Sunday Times* reported, the application is like "buying a new car with manual transmission and lots of extras—you don't just want to drive it, you want to fool around with it to see what it can do."

• Let's start off by entering the website's URL: **http://www.30boxes.com**. In the main page, click on the text **Just Get Started**. This will take you through the basic registration procedures.

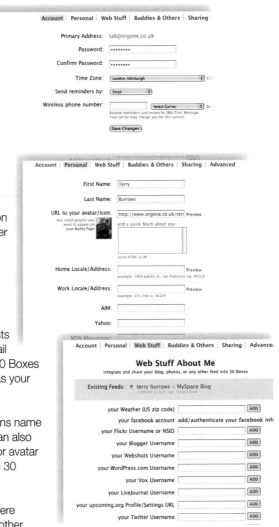

• Once your calendar page is set up, if you click on the **Settings** button on the top right-hand corner of the screen, you will find a number of tabbed pages in which you can set up or edit any of your personal information.

• The **Account** tab requests details regarding your e-mail address and password—30 Boxes uses your e-mail address as your principal form of identity.

• The **Personal** tab contains name and location details. You can also link to any external image or avatar that you want to use within 30 Boxes.

• The **Web Stuff** tab is where you can enter user IDs for other applications, such as MySpace, Blogger, and Flickr.

On the next page, we'll take a look at how you can set up contacts in the **Buddies & Others** tab.

Creating Buddies

One of the neatest aspects of 30 Boxes is how well the social networking features are integrated. Here we'll look at how to create contacts.

• Still working under **Settings**, click on the tab labeled **Buddies & Others**. In the section headed **Your Buddies**, click on **Add Buddy**.

• In the pop-up window, type the e-mail address you want to add. Here you can also set up how much of your private data you wish to share with this contact. Click on the **Add** button to create your new "buddy."

• Your new contact will now appear in the section headed **Your Buddies**.

Add an Event to Your Calendar

Now let's take a look at your main calendar page. To do this, click on the calendar icon—the box displaying the number "30"—on the top left-hand corner of the window. The calendar will now appear.

• To add an event to your calendar, highlight the day in question and then click on the **Add** button near the top of the window.

• The **Add a New Event** window will appear. Enter a name for the event, a time, and any descriptive notes you wish to include. If it is a meeting involving one of your 30 Boxes buddies, click on the box marked **Invites**, and a drop-down list showing all the e-mail addresses of all your buddies will appear. Select one of them from the list. Finally, click on the **Update Event** button to complete the operation. A confirmation window will appear—this

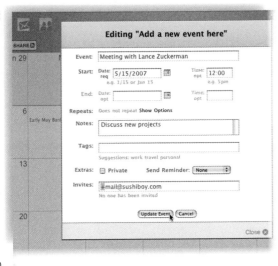

indicates that the software has sent an e-mail to your buddy, but he or she has not yet responded.

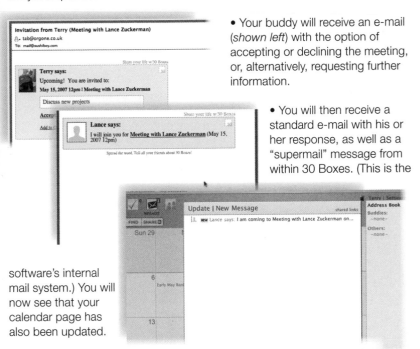

• Your buddy will receive an e-mail (*shown left*) with the option of accepting or declining the meeting, or, alternatively, requesting further information.

• You will then receive a standard e-mail with his or her response, as well as a "supermail" message from within 30 Boxes. (This is the

software's internal mail system.) You will now see that your calendar page has also been updated.

Other Time and Task Management Systems

Now let's take a brief look at some other calendar, project management, and to-do list applications.

HipCal

http://www.hipcal.com

HipCal is online calendar system developed in 2005 by a bunch of young entrepreneurs—five undergraduate fraternity brothers at Rensselaer Polytechnic Institute (RPI) in Troy, New York. It combines standard calendar features with a to-do list and will send out event alerts to e-mail addresses or cell phones. It's especially strong for creating a group calendar for team or class projects.

MeetWithApproval

http://www.meetwithapproval.com

The product of UK-based design company This Side Up, MeetWithApproval is a simple web-based application that enables users to arrange meetings or events, work out which day is convenient for those invited, and keep track of

who will be attending. It's extremely easy to use: the person creating the event completes a standard online form that creates a meeting page. Friends or colleagues are notified of the event via e-mail. They visit the meeting page and agree on a date. When everyone is happy, Meet With Approval confirms the arrangement.

Remember the Milk

http://www.rememberthemilk.com

Remember the Milk is one of the more popular task-management web-based applications. It features an extremely user-friendly interface, and—thanks to an extensive set of keyboard shortcuts—can also be quite swift to use.

It's possible to have event reminders sent out using a variety of different means: e-mail, SMS texts, instant messenger (AIM, Gadu-Gadu, Google Talk, ICQ, Jabber, MSN, Skype, and Yahoo!). It's also possible to tag lists and look at outstanding tasks as an overview "cloud." A weekly planner can be printed out, showing tasks for completion during the week ahead. The calendar can also be viewed with Apple iCal or Google Calendar. Any changes can be noted via RSS/ATOM feeds.

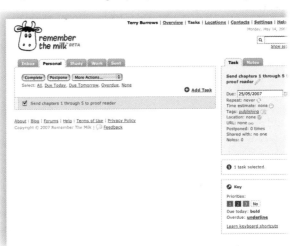

Ta-Da List

http://www.tadalist.com

A small Chicago-based company with the intriguing name of 37 Signals (which was so named after the 37 radio-telescope signals identified by astronomer Paul Horowitz as possible messages from extraterrestrial life forms) is responsible for a number of interesting applications using Ruby On Rails technology. The company's flagship product is the sophisticated project management tool Basecamp (**http://www.basecamphq.com**), for which users pay monthly fees for varying levels of service. However, they are also responsible for the free task management application Ta-Da List.

The user sets up a list with any number of tasks within. As tasks are completed, check boxes are ticked. Lists can also be shared with other users who can edit the contents.

• Enter the URL: **http://www.tadalist. com**. To get started, click on the text labeled **Create a New List**.

• Name your list—type your text in the box and then click on the **Create This List** button.

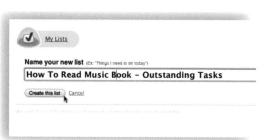

• In the page that follows, enter the name of a task and then click on **Add This Item**. Continue until you have set up all of your tasks within the list.

• You can now view your complete list. As you complete tasks you can tick them off by clicking on the check boxes to the left of each one. You can also e-mail a copy of the list to yourself or be notified via an RSS feed of changes made to your list. The contents of the list can be modified or added to at any time by

How To Read Music Book - Outstanding Tasks

Proof chapters 1 to 4.

+ Add this item   Close

You can also...
• Be notified of changes to this list via RSS: **RSS**
• Email yourself a copy of this list.

clicking on the **Edit** button above the list.

Sharing Your Ta-Da List

To share a list, click on the button marked **Share**. You have two different sharing options. The first is to enter one or more e-mails and then click on the button labeled **Share with These People**. You can also add a note that will appear in the body text of the e-mail. Take care to note that

My Lists **This list:** Edit | Reorder | Share

How To Read Music Book - Outstanding Tasks

☐ Proof chapters 1 to 4
☐ Proof chapters 5 to 8
☐ Check all music artworks
☐ Complete Glossary
☐ Hand over to indexer by end of month
  Add another item

you are not only giving these individuals permission to look at your list, but also to *change* anything on your list. This is ideal for project lists where actions are to be taken by different individuals.

A second share option open to you is to tick the **Yes, Share Publicly** checkbox. This enables anyone to view your list, although they will not be able to make any changes themselves.

Taskfreak!

http://www.taskfreak.com

This is a suite of three open-source personal management web applications, comprising separate task management, time tracking, and project management functions. The applications are also optimized for use with mobile devices.

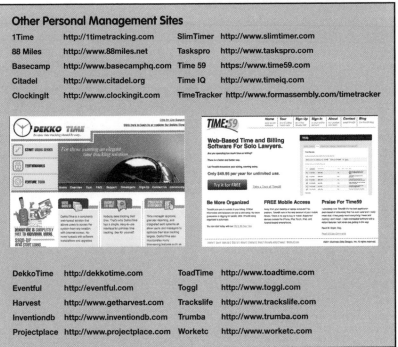

Other Personal Management Sites

1Time	http://1timetracking.com	SlimTimer	http://www.slimtimer.com
88 Miles	http://www.88miles.net	Taskspro	http://www.taskspro.com
Basecamp	http://www.basecamphq.com	Time 59	https://www.time59.com
Citadel	http://www.citadel.org	Time IQ	http://www.timeiq.com
ClockingIt	http://www.clockingit.com	TimeTracker	http://www.formassembly.com/timetracker
DekkoTime	http://dekkotime.com	ToadTime	http://www.toadtime.com
Eventful	http://eventful.com	Toggl	http://www.toggl.com
Harvest	http://www.getharvest.com	Trackslife	http://www.trackslife.com
Inventiondb	http://www.inventiondb.com	Trumba	http://www.trumba.com
Projectplace	http://www.projectplace.com	Worketc	http://www.worketc.com

Photographs and Videos

As consumer broadband speeds continue to increase, home computers inevitably will be better equipped to rival television as a medium of entertainment. Nowhere has this been better demonstrated than with the massive success of the video-sharing site YouTube. Although nominally a place where people can share their homemade videos, it owes much of its growth and success to users illegally uploading commercial content—sometimes complete feature films—and thus creating a massive online video database. In turn, record labels, TV and film companies, and other content owners have viewed YouTube as a fertile ground for free advertising. YouTube and its photographic equivalents, such as Flickr, also incorporate social networking dimensions, with users able to leave comments on each other's offerings, recommend pages to other users, and perform searches based on "folksonomous" category tags that they've created themselves.

Flickr

http://www.flickr.com

By any measure the world's most popular photo-sharing website, Flickr was launched in 2004 by Ludicorp, a company based in Vancouver, Canada. The application evolved out of a proposed multiuser game that was never released. Flickr first appeared as part of a chat room called FlickrLive, a place where users were able to exchange photographs.

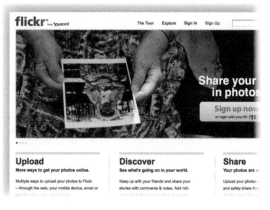

At this stage it was primarily a forum for sharing images collected from the Web. However, it quickly evolved as a means for users to show their own photography, and, in fact, the chat room itself was eventually dropped. Flickr's enormous popularity was soon followed by the the inevitable corporate buy-out—in March 2005 Ludicorp was acquired by the Yahoo! company.

The premise behind Flickr is extremely simple: users may upload their own photographs for others to view. To aid searches, multiple tags can be applied to any photograph. Images can also be grouped in collections known as "sets." Although it's possible for anyone to view Flickr images, registered users can also leave comments on specific photographs or even give them "favorite" ratings. It's also very easy to use.

Flickr is is used by some as a public gallery for their work—professional media, such as photo libraries, newspapers, and magazines often use Flickr as a source for picture research, so there is potential for users to earn income. Others may treat Flickr as a free means of cloud data storage.

Searching Flickr

Let's now look at Flickr in a little more detail. Begin by registering or logging in. We'll start off by performing a simple search operation.

• Enter the URL: **http://www.flickr.com**. In this example, we'll look for pictures that have the words **Aldeburgh Cinema** either as tags or in titles and descriptive text. Type this into the **Search** box in the top right-hand corner of the screen. From the drop-down menu, click on **Search Everyone's Uploads**.

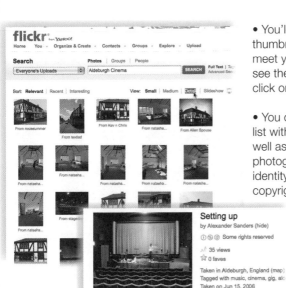

• You'll now see a list of thumbnail views of images that meet your search criteria. To see them in an enlarged form, click on the **Detail** button.

• You can now see the same list with enlarged images, as well as information about the photograph, such as title, identity of the photographer, copyright details, the location it was taken, any tags that have been applied, how many other Flickr users have viewed it, and the number of "fave" ratings it has received. You can use the scroll bar to view other matching images.

Setting up
by Alexander Sanders (hide)
Some rights reserved
35 views
0 faves
Taken in Aldeburgh, England (map)
Tagged with music, cinema, gig, al
Taken on Jun 15, 2006

Stage left
by Alexander Sanders (hide)
Some rights reserved
64 views
0 faves
Taken in Aldeburgh, England (map)

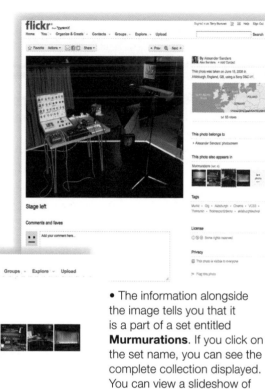

• If you now want to look at a full-size version of the photograph, click on the thumbnail view. As you can see, this image has been given eight different category tags. (In fact, it's possible to allocate up to 75 tags to any one photograph.) You can also see a map that plots precisely where the photograph was taken.

• The information alongside the image tells you that it is a part of a set entitled **Murmurations**. If you click on the set name, you can see the complete collection displayed. You can view a slideshow of the set by clicking on the text labeled **View as Slideshow**.

Uploading Photographs

To put a picture on Flickr, first make sure that the images are ready on your hard drive. Any of the standard file formats (JPEG, PNG, non-animated GIF, BMP, and TIFF) are allowable. Before you can upload photographs to the Flickr website, you need to create a Yahoo! account for yourself. On the Flickr homepage, click on the **Sign Up Now!** button and follow the instructions.

• When you've set up your ID and password, sign in to Flickr. Click on the **Upload** button.

• You will be taken to the Flickr upload page. Click on the button labeled **Choose Photos and Videos** (Flickr also allows you to load small—less than 90 seconds—video clips.)

• You can upload up to six photographs at one time. Begin by locating the first image on your hard drive using the browse

window. Highlight the file name and click on the **Open** button.

• The **Upload to Flickr** window will appear, listing the name of the image you chose to upload. You now have the choice of adding further images (click on **Add More**) or finishing there. Before making the file transfer, however, you must decide

on your privacy settings. By clicking on the **Public** button, any Flickr user can view the image; the **Private** button allows you to make it visible only to family or friends. Finally, click on **Upload Photos and Videos**. When the transfer has been completed, you will receive a message/link— **Finished! Next: add a description, perhaps?** Click on this link.

• A new window opens up enabling you to give a title, description, and tags to your photograph. Type in your details and click on the **Save** button.

• Your photograph is now in place on your Flickr photostream.

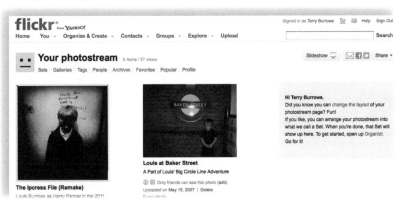

Enhancing Flickr

When a web application becomes massively successful, it's not unusual to find third parties prepared to provide services that aim to enhance their use. For example, there are numerous websites that will enable you to "pimp" your Facebook, MySpace, or other social networking sites. Similarly, there are those aimed at making the Flickr experience a little more interesting.

Flappr (http://bcdef.org/flappr)

Flappr offers an alternative way to search for and view images on the Flickr database. If you enter some search text, Flappr will provide a screen of thumbnail views along with a cloud of tags.

For a more detailed search, if you click on any tag, it will be added to your original search criteria and the list of thumbnails will be reduced. You can continue to add tags in this way. If you click on the image, it will appear full size on the right of the screen, accompanied by the profile of the photographer.

FlickrFling
(http://www.nastypixel.com)

FlickrFling provides a novel way of viewing Flickr photographs linked to popular news feeds. First select a news source from a drop-down list—in this example we have

chosen **CNN.com**. FlickrFling will take the current RSS feed and use each word as a key for a Flickr search. In this example, the feed reads **"Diana Nyad back in water after being stung by jellyfish…"** Some of the selections are extremely literal, but it does present an entertaining visual take on the news as it's coming in.

Slide

http://www.slide.com

Launched in 2005 by Max Levchin, one of the founders of PayPal, Slide claims to be the biggest independent "widget" company on the Internet. Slide is an application that enables the creation of customized slide shows of photographs that can be embedded in a blog or a social networking page, sent out as an RSS feed, or streamed to a desktop as a screensaver. As of May 2007, the company was claiming that more than 200,000 new slide shows were being created each day. Let's look at how simply a MySpace photo gallery can be customized using Slide.

• Begin by entering the URL: **http://www.slide.com**. Click on the button marked **Make a Slide Show**.

• In the list of options on the left-hand side of the screen, choose **MySpace**. Enter the MySpace URL that contains the photo gallery you wish to customize. Click on the **Get** button.

• You will see the images appearing in the window at the top of the screen. You can alter the "theme" of your slide show using the **Customize** options in the bottom right-hand corner of the screen. When you click on the **Save** button, Slide will save your slide show and also generate the HTML code that can then be copied and pasted into your MySpace page. Slide also links up in the same way with Facebook, Friendster, Bebo, Tagged, Flickr, and many others.

Smilebox

http://www.smilebox.com

Smilebox takes a slightly different approach to other photo-sharing websites. It enables users to upload their photographs and videos in order to create animated scrapbooks, photo albums, slideshows, postcards, and greetings cards. Smilebox features a large database of ready-made templates into which personal content can be dragged, dropped, edited, and customized. Once saved, Smilebox sends out e-mails to any contacts you've entered. They can then view your work. The basic Smilebox service is free. However, a monthly subscription buys you a greater choice of templates and other benefits.

SmugMug

http://www.smugmug.com

SmugMug is arguably the most professional photo-sharing website currently on the Internet. Both simple and attractive in design, its popularity among its users stems from the fact that it is free from advertising banners. The downside is that there is a subscription charge for even the basic service. However, for that cost, SmugMug does offer unlimited safe storage for your digital images—as the company itself proclaims, "It's like Fort Knox for your photos!"

SmugMug also offers a variety of other commercial services, such as professional-quality printing, as well as the option of buying T-shirts, playing cards, ceramics, mouse pads, mugs, aprons, and jigsaw puzzles all using your own images. Holders of a SmugMug "professional" account are also able to sell their photographs as digital downloads.

Webshots

http://www.webshots.com

Webshots was one of the first sucessful photo-sharing websites. It began in 1996 as a screensaver/ wallpaper site but later expanded into photo sharing. It is now one of the largest such communites on the Internet—by 2011, there were more than 687 million photographs on the site.

Copyright Issues

The term "copyright" refers to a set of laws that prevents the work of artists, authors, composers, or others from being used without permission. With regard to posting images, videos, or music on the Internet, although specific copyright laws vary from nation to nation, there is one basic rule that holds true pretty well everywhere: if you didn't create it yourself, then you probably don't have the legal right to upload it. So if you copy a video clip from the TV onto YouTube, you'll be in breach of copyright; the same rules apply if you upload photographs to Flickr that you didn't take yourself. Of course, this hasn't prevented a great many people from doing just that. (And it's fair to say that in some cases, copyright holders haven't objected strongly—especially where video clips have acted as advertising for more expensive products.) The bottom line is, whatever your reasons or excuses, you *are* breaking the law when you do this, and—however unlikely it may seem—you could be leaving yourself open to legal action. So always consider the possible risks before you upload illegal content!

YouTube

http://www.youtube.com

YouTube is a video sharing website where users may upload and view video clips. Videos may be given star ratings (to a maximum of five stars) and commented on by other viewers—an average rating and the number of times a video has been watched are both displayed as part of the video's details.

YouTube was created in 2005 by former employees of PayPal. Within its first year of operation, it had become the fastest growing site on the Internet, with over 100 million video clips being viewed daily. In October 2006, YouTube was acquired by Google for $1.65 billion worth of Google stock.

Much of the controversy relating to YouTube comes from users uploading copyrighted content. And the company has been the subject of numerous lawsuits from the major names in the television and film industries. However, as *Variety* magazine reported in March 2007, Hollywood has a complicated attitude toward the website: "The marketing guys love YouTube and the legal guys hate it." Legal threats have led the site to take a more proactive role in monitoring illegal activity. Yet it's fair to say that if you were to do a search for any well-known TV show you would still find plenty of content in place.

In September 2011, Alexa, the organization that measures web traffic, rated YouTube the third most visited site worldwide, behing Google and Facebook. The popularity of YouTube has heralded a new trend in viewing, especially among the young, where many are reputed to have turned away from traditional television in favor of watching TV content on their computers. As a result, TV companies are increasingly offering their programs in a downloadable format.

YouTube Search

There are a number of different ways you can find video content on YouTube. A simple text search is usually the best bet for finding specific content. However, since all videos may be given multiple tags, you can sometimes discover material of interest by performing category searches.

• Start by entering the URL: **http://www.youtube.com**. In this example, we'll look for video clips by the 1970s rock band **Gentle Giant**. Enter the text and click on the **Search** button.

• Next, you will find a list of all videos that fit your search criteria. Each video clip shows a thumbnail image from the start of the film, the title, any details the uploader has chosen to include, the category tags allocated to the clip, the name of the uploader, the number of times the clip has been viewed, the average star rating it has been given, and the number of viewers that have given a rating to the clip.

• You can watch the video by clicking on the title or the thumbnail image. It will appear in a new window at the top left-hand corner of the screen. You can control the video using the bar underneath the video clip.

To get the best out of YouTube, you need a reliable broadband connection that works at a reasonable speed, or else you'll get glitches and interruptions. This can also happen during periods of high traffic on popular clips.

The Transport Bar

Let's look briefly at what each of the controls on the transport bar can do.

The **Play** button is a toggle switch—when you click on it, the video will begin and the button will change its appearance, becoming a **Pause** button—if you click on the button again, the clip will be paused, and the button will revert to its original appearance. You can move to different parts of the video clip by dragging the cursor back and forth along progress bar. If you click on the **Full Screen** button the video will increase in size to fit your screen; the **Expand Screen** button fills out the screen widthways. The Video Resolution indicator tells you the technical quality of the clip—1080p represents a high-definition (HD) output. However, depending on the settings used or the quality of the source material, there's no guarantee that any clip won't turn out to be a jerky, bit-mapped mess that is nearly impossible to watch.

Search by Category

In the YouTube home page, if you click on the **Browse** tab near the top of the screen, the next page will give you the option of searching a set of predefined categories. If, for example, you click on Entertainment, you'll see a scrolling selection of the most popular clips that have been created with that tag.

Uploading Your Own Video Clip

Before you upload a video clip, first you need to ensure that it has been converted to a format that YouTube can understand, namely Windows Media Video (.wmv), Audio Video Interleave (.avi), Quicktime (.mov), or MPEG. To begin uploading, you must be a registered user and be logged in. If you are not a member, click on the **Sign Up** button at the top of the page and follow the registration instructions.

• On the YouTube home page, click the button marked **Upload**. The **Video File Upload** screen will appear. There are two ways that you can upload your

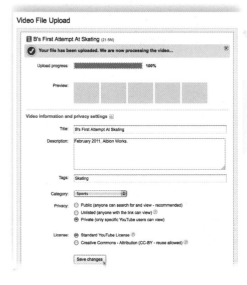

videos, either by clicking on the **Upload Video** button and browsing through your disk drive, or, if you have the file on your desktop, you can drag and drop the file into the box in the center of the screen.

• When the file has uploaded (or while the transfer is taking place), you can enter a title, description, tags, and privacy settings. (These can be set up so that, if you wish, only specific individuals can view.) When you have finished, click on **Save Changes**.

When the file has been uploaded, you will see a confirmation window. On this page you will find the URL of your clip to send to anyone you wish to view it. You will also find a scrolling box that contains the HTML coding that will create the links to your video. This can be embedded into a personal website, blog, or other applications, such as a MySpace page.

• If you return to your homepage and click on the arrow alongside your user ID, a drop-down menu headed **My Account** will appear. Click on the option marked **Videos**. You can now click on the title to watch the video.

Creating Your Own YouTube Channel

Avid YouTubers can create their own virtual TV channels, not only to show their own videos but also to share selections of public favorites. In the **My Account** drop-down menu, click on the **Subscriptions** option and complete the areas of the subsequent window that are relevant to you.

Vimeo

http://www.vimeo.com

Vimeo once was once as much about social networking as video sharing—a sort of hybrid of MySpace and YouTube. But in recent times, partially through its enablement of large, high-resolution video, it has carved a niche as the

site of choice for the more serious video maker. This is further borne out by the level of user comments, which tend to be more informed and constructive, and less juvenile in tone, than those found on YouTube.

Metacafe
http://www.metacafe.com

Founded in Israel but now based in California, Metacafe is unusual in that it was one of the first sites to pay users for posting popular videos. Once 20,000 people have viewed a video, Metacafe pays $5 for every one thousand views.

Break

http://www.break.com

Formed in 1998, Break is more focused in its content than other video sites, making its name for its comedy clips—particularly of the "blooper" variety. Social networking is very oriented toward 18-35 year-old males, and comments are often antagonistic—or rude. This demographic has made the site popular with advertisers and TV tie-ins. In fact, Break has teamed up with Endemol—the makers of *Big Brother* and *Fear Factor*—to produce original content.

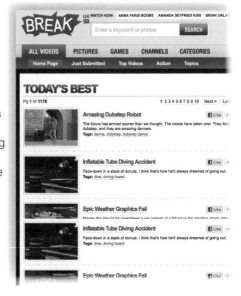

Stickam

http://www.stickam.com

Formed in 2005, Stickam is set apart from other video sharing sites by its extensive use of live video streaming, creating the equivalent of a video chat room. This technology was put to professional use when Stickam and Levi's partnered to stream MusicfestNW, the third largest indoor music festival in the USA. February 2010 saw the launch of Stickam Shuffle, a feature where users were able to connect instantly to random people from all over the world.

More Photograph and Video Sites

23hq	http://www.23hq.com	Stickam	http://www.stickam.com
Adultswim	http://www.adultswim.com	StupidVideos	http://www.stupidvideos.com
Blip.TV	http://www.blip.tv	Tagworld	http://www.tagworld.com
Broadbandsports	http://www.broadbandsports.com	Truveo	http://www.truveo.com
Clipshack	http://www.clipshack.com	Veoh	http://www.veoh.com
DailyMotion	http://www.dailymotion.com	Videobomb	http://videobomb.com
Dropshots	http://www.dropshots.com	Videoegg	http://www.videoegg.com
		VidiLife	http://www.vidilife.com
		Yahoo! Video	http://video.yahoo.com
		ZippyVideos	http://www.zippyvideos.com
		Zooomr	http://beta.zooomr.com/home
		Zoto	http://www.zoto.com

Flyinside	http://www.flyinside.com
Fotolia	http://www.fotolia.com
Google Video	http://video.google.com
Groupr	http://groupr.200ok.net
JumpCut	http://www.jumpcut.com
Mefeedia	http://www.mefeedia.com
Mightyv	http://www.mightyv.com
Phlog	http://phlog.net
Photobucket	http://www.photobucket.com
Photomap	http://photomap.mozdev.org
Revver	http://www.revver.com
Slidestory	http://www.slidestory.com

Podcasts

A podcast is an audio or video file that is distributed automatically to a subscribed user. That person can then play it back on a computer or mobile device, such as an mp3 player or cell phone. You could think of it as an Internet radio or TV show for which each episode is automatically delivered to the subscriber.

The Evolution of Podcasting

The word *podcast* was originally coined by the British technology writer Ben Hammersley in an article for the *Guardian* newspaper in 2004. It is a portmanteau of the words "iPod" and "broadcasting." However, you don't need an iPod to listen to a podcast; any mp3 player can be used. Apple, the manufacturer of the iPod, initially took legal steps to prevent the term being used commercially. But, when the editors of the *New Oxford American Dictionary* declared "podcasting" to be the word of the year in 2005, and thus gave it a definition—"a digital recording of a radio broadcast or similar program, made available on the Internet for downloading to a personal audio player"—there was clearly no going back.

Although the main technical developments took place in the United States, it was in the UK that the idea first achieved mainstream popularity when at the end of 2005 comedian Ricky Gervais began his own podcast show. It remains the most widely received podcast worldwide, with an average of around 300,000 downloads per episode. Gervais broke further ground a year later with his second series, which became the first major podcast to charge consumers for each download.

This "content-on-demand" idea is certain to evolve over the coming years and may provide a glimpse of how we receive our TV shows in the future. Recently, although podcasters have largely taken the traditional radio broadcast as a primary model, other approaches are slowly appearing.

Over the next few pages, we'll take a look at everything you need to subscribe and listen to a podcast, and also how you can go about creating and distributing your very own. Note: there is also some crossover here with the section on blogging—that's because a podcast is in essence an audio or video blog.

How It Works

On the surface, a podcast may seem

similar to other existing digital delivery technologies, such as downloading and streaming. The key difference, however, is that files are downloaded *automatically*. This is achieved using software that can read a *syndication feed*—a specific kind of data format used for providing the end user with content that changes frequently.

The mechanics of the process are easy to understand. The content provider creates a podcast "episode," which is usually an mp3 file, and references a syndication feed file, usually in RSS format. This is a list of the web URLs used to find specific podcast episodes. It is posted to the server at its permanent URL address. The podcaster then makes the feed known to his or her target audience.

The receiver uses a type of software known as an aggregator (or podcatcher) to subscribe to and manage his or her feeds. This is typically a program that launches when the computer is switched on and runs permanently in the background, periodically checking if feed data has changed. If it has, a new episode is automatically downloaded. This can then be heard using playback software or downloaded to an mp3 player or suitably equipped cell phone.

Podcasting: Other Uses

Music Replacement for live performance audio streams.

Adding content Enables news organizations to distribute audio or video to supplement or complement existing news.

Promotional tool Disney/Pixar famously trailed their film *Cars* with a series of video podcasts.

Avoiding regulatory bodies
Enables broadcasts that may not be allowed in traditional media.

Education Podcasts are increasingly used in universities and high schools as a way of disseminating lectures.

Commentary Alternative audio commentaries can accompany DVDs or TV shows. Podcasts have been made by the creators of popular shows to accompany specific episodes. There are also examples of fans providing their own commentaries to accompany releases.

Politics and religion Political parties have adopted the podcast as a way of reaching younger audiences. Some churches issue their own "Godcasts" of sermons and lectures.

Receiving a Podcast

There are three simple steps you need to take to receive a podcast. First you need some podcast software, then you need to subscribe to the podcast, and finally, you should select your medium for listening to or viewing the podcast.

Podcast Software

To begin, you will need to install a piece of software on your computer that is able to search the Web for podcasts, which will then automatically deliver the latest episode to your computer. Most of this software can be downloaded free of charge. The three most popular applications

are iTunes, Juice, and Doppler. You can find a more extensive list of other podcasting software on the next page.

iTunes

http://www.apple.com

There are a variety of ways you can subscribe to a podcast, some of which will depend on the software you use. Apple's iTunes (which works on PCs as well as Macs) is a popular choice, primarily because so many people use it to organize and play their music collections. You can download iTunes from the Apple website: **http://www.apple.com**. The software also doubles as a storefront for the company's highly successful commercial music and video download store.

Let's begin with a simple and common example of a podcast link found within a website. Here we'll look at Football Weekly, one of a number

of excellent podcasts produced by the British newspaper the *Guardian* as a means of providing additional news content. (In fact, the *Guardian* has an entire menu of podcasts as well as a hefty archive, many of which can be obtained free of charge through iTunes.)

Podcasting Software

Almost all of the software needed to capture and listen to podcasts is free to download. This is a small list of some of the better-known products. If you enter the name of the software into any search engine you will find links to where they can be downloaded. (Note: The letters in parentheses indicates the platforms on which the software operates: **L**—Linux; **M**—Mac; **W**—Windows.)

@Podder (W)	Client for the visually impaired.
BlogMatrix Sparks! (W)	Record, mix, share, publish, store, and listen to podcasts.
Doppler (W)	Podcast aggregator—a tool to subscribe to RSS feeds.
HappyFish (W)	Syncs podcasts to most mp3 players.
iPodderX (W/M)	Handles podcasts, vlogs, and other distributed files.
iTunes (W/M)	All-in-one downloading and listening solution.
Juice (W/M)	Enables users to select and automatically download pocasts.
NetNewsWire (M)	RSS and Atom newsreader for Mac OS X.
NewsFire (M)	Newsreader and podcast client.
NewsMacPro (M)	Supports podcasting and syncs with Palm and iPod.
Peapod (L)	Podcast client for Linux.
Poddumfeeder (M)	Applescript-based podcast client.
Podspider (W)	Podcast client with integrated podcast directory.
Replay Radio (W)	Captures podcasts, broadcast radio shows, and XM Radio.
RSSRadio (W)	Podcasting software for Windows.
Synclosure (W)	RSS aggregator.
TVTonic (W)	A video podcast reader optimized for Windows Media Center.
WinAmp (W/M)	Commercial audio application with free "iite" option.
Yamipod (W/M/L)	iPod management.

• Go to the *Guardian*'s **Audio & Podcasts** page by entering the URL **http://www.guardian.co.uk/audio**. Scroll down the page and select a podcast from the list. This will take you to the podcast's own homepage.

• If you look at the transport bar, you'll see several options. If you click on the Play icon, you can listen to the podcast. The three text buttons beneath provide a variety of download options. Rather than download a single podcast, let's subscribe, which means all subsequent episodes will be delivered automatically. Click on **Subscribe Free via iTunes**.

• This opens up the podcast's iTunes **Preview** page. This lists all of the episodes of Football Weekly that are currently available. For the most recent episode, click on the button marked **View In iTunes**.

• This will automatically launch iTunes. (For this to work, you must, of course, already have downloaded and installed the iTunes software on your computer, tablet, or smartphone.) You will then see the podcast's header page, with a description of its content, episode details, and viewer/listener reviews. Guardian podcasts are free of charge, so click on the button marked **Subscribe Free**.

• If you now look in the Podcast section of your iTunes library, the most recent episode of the podcast you subscribed to will have been downloaded. You will also see that, in this example, you have been notified of a number of earlier episodes. If you want to download any or all of these,

you need to click on the **Get** button. From this point, each time you launch iTunes when connected to the Internet, your computer will search for new episodes of that podcast.

Juice

http://juicereceiver.sourceforger.net

We'll now look at subscribing to a podcast using a piece of aggregator software. In this example we'll use a popular free program called Juice.

Begin by downloading the software from the URL above. Install it on your computer.

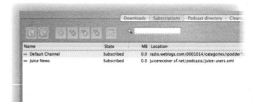

When you launch the program for the first time, Juice will open up with a pair of default subscriptions (*see the bottom of the previous page*). Juice also has a useful podcast directory, which lists numerous broadcasts from various global sources.

• Click on the button marked **Podcast Directory**. The podcasts are grouped within folders; double-click on any folder to see what is available inside. In this example, we've chosen the archive of **Adam Curry's Pod Squad**—a list of favorites selected by the so-called Podfather himself.

• Let's download **The Rock and Roll Geek Show** by double-clicking on the title. You will see the URL of the feed appearing in the box near the top of the window. To subscribe to that podcast, click on the **Save** button.

• If you click on the **Downloads** tab and look in the column headed **State**, you will see that your selected podcast is indeed being transferred to your computer. The column named **Progress** indicates how much of the file has been downloaded so far, and the current speed of the transfer. When the file has arrived on your hard drive, you can play it using your chosen mp3 software or transfer it to an external mp3 player or a suitably equipped cell phone.

Adding Your Own Podcast Choices

Directories like those found in Juice and similar types of software are all well and good for introducing you to selections of the most popular podcasts, but in most cases you are going to want to subscribe to the ones that you find for yourself or that are recommended to you by others. To incorporate these into Juice, you first need to add the "feed" of the podcast manually. (The feed is the URL address the software will go to each time it wants to look for a new episode.)

There are many places you can look around for podcast feeds—most news and entertainment websites will have plenty. There are also numerous web-based podcast directories. When you find your chosen podcast, it will usually be accompanied by a button labeled something like **Subscribe**. (The widely used orange-colored XML button is also commonly used for podcast feeds.)

• In this example, we'll use a web directory called Podcast Alley. Enter the URL—**http:// www.podcastalley. com**. You can use a keyword search or browse through categories to find podcasts. When you've located the podcast that interests you—in this case, the comedy show **Am I Bugging You?**—click on the **Subscribe** button.

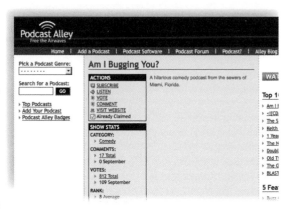

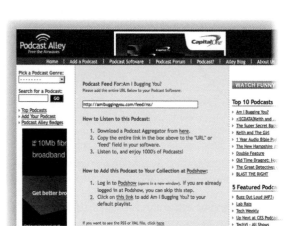

• The box that opens offers a variety of possibilities for subscription, including the URL for the feed. Highlight and copy the URL in the box. (**Command + C** for Macs; **Ctrl + C** for PCs.)

• Launch the Juice application. From the **Tools** menu, select **Add a Feed**.

• In the **Add a Feed** pop-up window, click on the empty box labeled **URL**. Paste the URL into the box. (**Command + V** for Macs; **Ctrl + V** for PCs.) At the same time, you also have the option of entering your own title and description for the podcast.

• To complete the subscription, click on the **Save** button.

• The selected

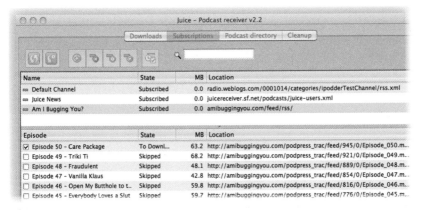

podcast now appears in Juice's download list. In the bottom half of the window, you can view the available episodes of the podcast. Once the episode has been transferred, you can play the file on your computer or copy it to your tablet, smartphone, or mp3 player.

Podcasting Directory

The list below represents a small sample of the podcast (and video podcast) directories available on the Internet. Although most cover a wide array of categories, some are more specialized in their content.

All Podcasts	http://www.allpodcasts.com	General
AmigoFish	http://www.amigofish.com	General
Digital Podcast	http://www.digitalpodcast.com	Entertainment
EveryPodcast.com	http://www.everypodcast.com	General
fluctu8.com	http://www.fluctu8.com	General
HardPodCafe	http://hardpodcafe.com	General
iPodderX	http://ipodderx.com	General
Learn Out Loud	http://www.learnoutloud.com	Education
New Time Radio	http://newtimeradio.com	Comedy
Nutsie	http://nutsie.com	Music and cell phone content
Phonecasting	http://www.phonecasting.com	Cell phone
Podcast Alley	http://www.podcastalley.com	General
Podcast Blaster	http://www.podcastblaster.com	General
Podcast Central	http://www.podcastcentral.com	Podcast charts
Podcast Directory	http://www.podcastdirectory.com	General
Podcast Empire	http://www.podcastempire.com	Directory, forum, and blog
PodcastPickle	http://www.podcastpickle.com	Rated content
Podcast Pup	http://podcastpup.com	General
Revision3	http://revision3.com	Video
StreetIQ	http://streetiq.com	Business/finance
Zencast	http://www.zencast.com	General

Creating Your Own Podcast

There are two distinct phases in making your own podcast. The first step is to create the audio or video file that you want to broadcast; the second is to upload your podcast file to a specific location and then let the world know how to get hold of it.

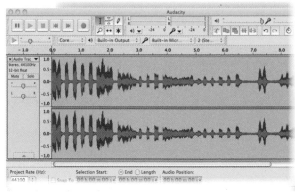

Writing and recording a podcast is well outside the scope of a book such as this—the best we can come up with is a list of basic commonsense tips listed later in this section. That said, most modern-day laptops come equipped with basic sound-recording equipment and often featured in-built video cameras. There is also plenty of freely available software on the internet on which you can record and edit your podcasts—such as Audacity (*see above*). However, if

you are interested, there is a huge amount of information on this topic to be found on the Internet. The remainder of this segment assumes you have already recorded your podcast and are happy with its content.

Uploading Your Own Podcast

For anyone to watch or listen to your podcast, it must first be uploaded to a location on the Internet that can be accessed by the public. In other words, it needs its own exclusive address. If you have your own website or access to an FTP server, this is very straightforward: all you need to do is create a folder in your "public" area and upload the file to that folder. When you've done that, make a note of the full URL of the file you've copied across. (It's likely to be something like **http://www.yourdomain.com/podcasts/myveryimportantpodcastepisode1.mp3**.)

If you don't have an FTP server, you'll need to find a site that will host your podcast on your behalf. There are a number of free or cheap options here that we'll look at shortly. However, there are two critical issues that we should first address: server space and bandwidth.

Server Space

The amount of server space you need for the storage of your podcasts will depend on four critical factors:

- The length of each episode
- The audio quality of your mp3 files
- How often you produce episodes
- How many episodes you want to make available at any time

If you were to use standard CD-quality digital audio for your podcast, the files would be much too large for most subscribers to download quickly. This is why podcast audio files are "compressed" in the mp3 format. (And, indeed, this is the reason that mp3, for all its sonic limitations, is so hugely popular.) Compression enables files to be reduced to a tenth of their size without too drastic a drop in sound quality. This also means that upload and download times are reduced by a similar factor. The key component here is the "bit rate" of the audio file, which you are able to set when you create your final mp3 file. The rule here is simple: the higher the bit rate, the better the sound, but the larger the file. So it's all a matter of balancing trade-offs. As far as podcasters are concerned, 128 kilobytes per second would be adequate for most music; for spoken word, 64 or 96 kilobytes per second should work. This means that:

- A 128 kbps stereo file will take up around 1 megabyte/minute
- A 96 kbps stereo file will take up around 0.7 megabytes/minute

So if, for example, you were to create a 30-minute stereo podcast using a bit rate of 96 kbps, each episode would take around 21 megabytes of storage space. If you were to record one episode each week and wanted make a year's worth of episodes available online at all times, you would need 1,092 megabytes—or just over a gigabyte—of server space. Many hosting services will offer a limited basic package of up to a gigabyte and then charge incrementally for larger amounts of space.

Bandwidth

The second major factor to consider when choosing a server for your podcasts is the bandwidth. This is the amount of data that your host server allows to be transferred back and forth each month. Each time you upload a podcast, some of your bandwidth allowance will be used; more significantly, each time anyone downloads your podcast, that *also* will eat into your allowance. If your podcasts suddenly start becoming popular, then you must ensure that your host allows you enough bandwidth to accommodate your audience, otherwise, depending on the deal you have with your host, you may have to pay excessive fees, or you may find that your account is frozen or removed. If this thought seriously worries you and you have ambitions of reaching a large audience, you really need to look for a host server that offers you unlimited bandwidth.

So how do you assess your likely monthly bandwidth requirement? The calculation itself is a very simple piece of arithmetic but is made very difficult by one simple fact: you have to estimate how many people are going to attempt to download your podcast. Once you're up and running you'll quickly get a feel for the size of your audience, but to begin with you really just have to guess! So, for example, if our 21-megabyte podcast is downloaded by 200 people in a month, and one episode is issued every week, then a monthly bandwidth of 16.8 gigabytes would be needed. As with space, if you want a lot of bandwidth, you'll have to pay for it.

Simple Hosting

Selecting the best place to host a podcast will depend on how seriously you intend to take your podcasting. If you just want to give it a try, and don't envision doing it very frequently, you should be able to find a free solution. Let's take a look at one of these services—PodBean.

PodBean

http://www.podbean.com

PodBean is a typical podcast host and directory. It offers a basic package, which is free, with allowances of 100 megabytes of storage and 5 gigabytes bandwidth. (As you can see, the weekly podcast example we outlined above would already be struggling here.) There are a number of other packages offering unlimited storage and bandwidth for a small monthly charge.

• Enter the URL: **http://www.podbean.com**. First you must register as a user: to do this, click on the **Sign-Up** label and follow the instructions. Once you've registered you can log in.

• To begin uploading, click on the **Publish a Podcast** tab.

• PodBean recommends that you begin by filling out details of the podcast that will appear in your menu (*see above right*). Click on the button marked **Add Your Audio/Video**.

• A new box will open: click on the text labeled **Upload New Files**.

• The **Media Manager** page will open. Click on **Upload** and then the button marked **Choose File**.

• Navigate through your hard drive until you find your podcast file, and click on the **Choose** button. Finally, click on the **Upload** button. Your podcast will now transfer to the PodBean server.

• If you click on the **Layout** tab, you will be able to select

a "theme." This is the layout and text style that others will see when they discover your podcast.

This page contains a number of different designs—scroll down the list to view all the options. To make your choice, click on the title above the thumbnail image. You can see how your page will look by clicking on **View Site**—a small piece of text that appears next to your username near the top of the screen.

• Your podcast has now been uploaded.

Accessing Your Podcast

This is how your podcast page will look to another user. They will also be able to comment on and rate what you have done. And they can contact you using PodBean's internal mail system.

• The podcast will become available when a user clicks on the **Subscribe** button. This will open their **My Subscriptions** page, which gives an overview of all subscribed podcasts, along with their average ratings.

• If you click on the orange **RSS** button (it appears alongside the podcaster's ID), this will open a new page, which gives the option of adding that podcast to a number of popular "podcatcher" programs. The box beneath shows the URL of your podcast feed. This can be copied and pasted into other podcast software, in the same way we did with Juice.

Good Podcasting Tips

What's your point? If your podcast is themed, follow the three classic rules of public speaking: say what you're going say; say it; and then say what you just said.

Keep it short We've all got short attention spans these days—15 to 30 minutes should be ample for most podcasts.

Structure There may be a few gifted individuals who can switch on a microphone and talk engagingly for 30 minutes without much preparation, but if you or I try it, the results are sure to be mind-numbingly bad. Structure your program so that it can be broken into smaller chunks. If you are interviewing someone, prepare the questions in advance.

Create an identity Every TV and radio show has a theme tune that heralds its arrival and departure. Your podcast should be no different.

Technical quality Recording audio is a skill in its own right. But while lo-fi sound has its place in popular culture, having to endure a tinny, hissy, crackly, low quality podcast can be a painful experience. While most computers can record high quality digital audio, almost any built-in microphone will sound poor. Invest in, or borrow, a reasonable microphone and a pop screen to prevent those "P" syllables from leaping out.

Quiet Unless you are specifically doing an on-location podcast, always do your microphone recording in quiet surroundings. You don't want to hear traffic noise, dogs barking, or your family talking in the background.

Edit before broadcast Most computers now come equipped with some kind of basic digital sound-editing software. If yours does not, try Audacity, which is cross-platform, open-source, and free (**http://audacity.sourceforge.net**). Use it to construct and edit your podcast. Study other radio shows or podcasts that you like, listening for production techniques such as using background music for transitions.

Identify your podcast If you plan to podcast regularly, it may be a good idea to begin your program with some "meta" information, such as date, epsidode number, and subject. This will give an overall sequence to your shows.

Easy listening Make it as easy as possible for users to subscribe.

Creating an RSS Feed

As we have seen in the example above, hosts such as PodBean can offer an appealing all-in-one solution to the different processes required to launch a podcast. However, there will be other occasions when you may need to do things manually—for example, if you are creating a feed for your own website. So let's now look at some other ways of creating a feed.

Really Simple Syndication

To begin with, what exactly *is* an RSS feed? RSS is an acronym for **Really Simple Syndication** and is one of a number of web feed formats used to publish frequently updated digital content. This not only includes podcasts, but also blogs and news feeds as well. In simple terms, you could think of an RSS feed as a table of contents. The feed does not itself contain the podcast, but links to it using its URL. While RSS is by far the most widely used type of feed, it is by no means the only one. ATOM, another XML-based feed, is rated more highly by the technical community. However, there are certain compatibility issues between the two, so, as far as podcasters are concerned, they need only worry about RSS for the time being.

An RSS feed is a text file created using a language called XML (Extensible Markup Language). Anyone familiar with XML can easily create his or her own feed files—it's not terribly difficult and not that different from the HTML used in website design. However, an alternative approach—and one strongly recommended here—is that if you *have* to create your own feed files, then make life a little easier by using one of the many online RSS generator websites. Two good examples are Podcast Generator (**http://www.tdscripts.com**) and Listgarden (**http://www.softwaregarden.com/products/listgarden**). Both of these sites work in a similar way: you input the required information into the table and then click on a button to generate the coding to paste into a simple text file.

podcast RSS feed generator - use this the very first time you create a new RSS 2.0 podcast	
Blog / Website Title	My Really Important Podcast
Blog / Website URL	http://orgone.co.uk/podcast/feed
Blog / Website Description	Episode Title
Language	English
Copyright info	Terry Burrows
Webmaster email address	tab@orgone.co.uk
Enclosure title	Episode 1
Enclosure description	First Episode of Mt Really Important Podcast
Enclosure link	http://www.orgone.co.uk/podcast/mypodcast1.mp3
Enclosure type (audio/mpeg)	MP3
Enclosure size (in bytes)	4834743
	Create RSS 2.0 feed (first time)

```
<?xml version="1.0"?>
  <rss version="2.0">
    <channel>
      <title>My Really Important Podcast</title>
      <link>http://orgone.co.uk/podcast/feed</link>
      <description>Episode Title</description>
      <language>en-us</language>
      <copyright>Terry Burrows</copyright>
      <lastBuildDate>Wed, 23 May 2007 09:16:53 GMT<
      <generator>tdscripts.com Podcast Generator</gene
<webMaster>tab@orgone.co.uk</webMaster>
      <ttl>1</ttl>
      <item>
        <title>Episode 1</title>
        <description>First Episode of Mt Really Important
        <pubDate>Wed, 23 May 2007 09:16:53 GMT</p
        <enclosure url="http://www.orgone.co.uk/podcas
length="4834743" type="audio/mpeg"/>
      </item>
    </channel>
  </rss>
```

Ensure that you save the file with a suffix of ".rss" and then upload the file to your website. This is the file that then needs to be linked to an RSS button on your website, passed on to podcast directories, or just given out to anyone interested in receiving your podcast.

Before promoting your podcast, there's one more thing you need to do: check that your feed is working. Once again, there are a number of free web applications to help you with this. For example, go to **http://rss.scripting.com**, enter the URL address of your RSS file, and click on the **Validate** button. If you get an error message, then there is something wrong with your XML coding.

Promoting Your Podcast

With millions of other podcasters busy doing their thing all over the Internet, you can't simply expect to upload your program and suddenly find yourself with a massive audience. That means taking every opportunity possible to publicize what you are doing. So here are some ideas to help you reach a greater number of listeners and viewers.

Podcast directories   We've already seen the importance of podcasting directories as a source of available content. As a podcaster, it's *critically* important that you register your work with the main podcast directories. Inclusion in podcast search engines and directories will open up a potentially enormous audience. You can find a massive selection of directories to contact at **http://www.podcasting-tools.com/submit-podcasts.htm**. This may be daunting and tedious work, but it's vitally important.

iTunes   Getting your podcast listed with iTunes will be the single most significant step you can take. Unfortunately, since the acceptance process is somewhat subjective, there is no guarantee that this will happen. Apple has produced its own guide, which you're strongly recommended to study: **http://www.apple.com/itunes/podcasts/specs.html**.

Let people know   Send something resembling a press release about your podcast to absolutely anyone who you think may be interested in what you have to say. If you have a social networking site, send out a bulletin or message to all your friends.

Look the part   Add suitable images to your website that will let visitors know that a podcast is available. Popular icons include the orange rectangles used to indicate RSS feeds, but many others are now used. A nice selection of free downloadable podcast icons is available from **http://www.feedforall.com /podcasting-graphics.htm**.

Be descriptive   People browsing websites rarely read every word in front of them, so make sure that your RSS feed contains the kind of keyword information that will grab the interest of potential listeners.

Educate your listeners   Remember that podcasting is a relatively new idea: there may be a large potential audience out there made up of people who have little or no understanding of what podcasting is all about, let alone how to subscribe to one. Therefore it may be worth your while to explain on your website a little about the nature of podcasting, or at least create a link to a podcasting FAQ site, such as **http://www.podcastingnews.com.**

Participate   Comment and interact with other podcaster's websites. Particularly, those that have commonalities with your own podcast. Make sure to include a link to your podcast in your signature.

Portals

A portal is a website that acts as a centralized point of information and contains links to other significant or related webpages. Business organizations have long understood their significance—they represent a first point of online contact and so are an important part of the modern branding process. A portal has a slightly different meaning for most individual users. Here it generally refers to a user-defined home page that appears each time a browser is launched. While it would be possible to program a custom-made webpage according to your own needs, there are now many simpler solutions available.

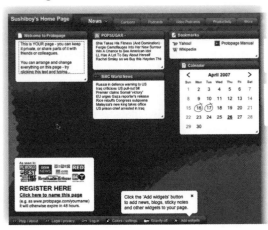

Your Own Front Page

So what do you want to see on your screen when you first launch your browser? In the past, the most common approach was to set the browser preferences to a preferred search engine or news page. In recent times, however, the "dashboard" approach has become increasingly popular. This is a type of portal that is made up of what are called "widgets"—each of which can be an individual application in its own right. Examples of widgets include calendars, diaries, news items, search engines, weather reports, and games. The key factor here is that the *specific* content and appearance is defined by the user.

iGoogle Homepage

http://www.google.com/ig

Let's look at one of the most popular user-definable portals—Google's personal home page. This brings an assortment of functions from across the Web into a single page, while keeping the popular search engine feature in place.

• Begin by typing in the URL **http://www.google.com/ig**. The screen that appears is the default homepage.

• The screen comprises a number of individual windows: Google has renamed these widgets as "gadgets." Each window can be repositioned around the screen by clicking and dragging on the menu bar. When a gadget is selected, you will see the settings "cog" icon on its top right-hand corner. In this example we'll look at Google's **Weather** gadget. If you click on the icon, a drop-down menu will appear. Choose **Edit Settings**. The top of half of the gadget now opens up with assorted editing options, such as switching between temperature scales and adding a new current location. Click on the **Save** button when you have made your changes.

Adding Gadgets to Your Homepage

Let's now take a look at how easy it is to customize your home page. Google itself offers a great number of options, from Google Maps and Gmail to puzzles and games. Additionally, there is an ever-growing list of third-party widgets available. First, though, let's actually make it into your browser homepage.

• Click on the text marked **Make iGoogle My Homepage**. (You can find it beneath the search box near the top of the page.) A window will appear asking you to drag a link to the browser's "home" icon—the little house in the top right-hand corner. Every time you open a new window in your browser this is the first page you will see.

• Let's now look into adding some new gadgets to your homepage. On the top left-hand side of the screen, click on the **Add Gadgets** button.

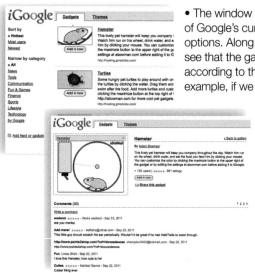

• The window that opens contains a list of Google's current most popular gadget options. Along the left of screen you can see that the gadgets have been organized according to their categories. In this example, if we click on the **Fun & Games** category we'll see the "hottest" entries listed.

• You can click on the titles of any gadget to find more information. Here we'll take a look at a gadget called Hamster, which simply shows a never-ending animation of hamster running in a wheel—it doesn't do much, it's just a bit of fun!

• If you want to activate the gadget, click on the **Add It Now** button beneath the preview screen. When you've done that, the button will turn orange and the text will change to **Added**.

• Finally, to see what your new gadget looks like, click on **Back To iGoogle Home**.

Adding a Theme

You can customize the look of your home page by adding what is called a "theme." This alters design aspects of the page—color, layout, images—without changing the content.

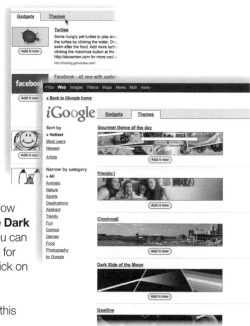

• To call up the list of options, click on the **Add Gadget** button and then on the **Themes** tab. The selection will appear in a window on the page. Let's choose the **Dark Side of the Moon** theme. You can either click on one of the titles for more information, or simply click on **Add It Now**.

• You can now see the effect this has on your homepage.

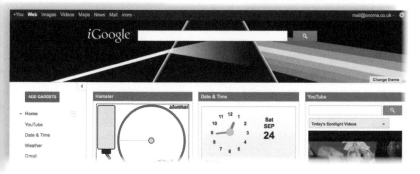

Netvibes

http://www.netvibes.com

Netvibes was founded in 2005 in Paris, France. Whereas Google's Personal Homepage is aimed squarely at the average Internet user, the AJAX-based Netvibes portal is perhaps more specialized in its appeal. It works in broadly the same way—a series of user-defined modules—but also incorporates RSS feeds, podcasts, and a limited social networking capability, in that you can send recommendations to other users or e-mail them to friends. Many of these modules can also be integrated into your own websites using html commands.

• Enter the URL **http://www.netvibe. com**. A default home page will load. To alter to the content of your page, click on the button marked **Add Content**.

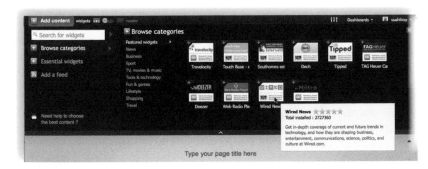

• The top of the screen opens out. From the list on the left, select **Browse Categories**. Here you can work through pages of the most popular Netvibe modules. When your mouse moves over one of the icons, a pop-up window will appear giving you a brief description of the widget, telling you how many other

users have downloaded it and the average rating (out of five stars). Here we have selected the gadget for the technology magazine *Wired*.

• If you click on widget's icon, a preview window will open. To install the widget on your Netvibes homepage, click on **Add to My Page**.

- The gadget is now installed on your homepage.

Reader Mode

The information for many of Netvibe's gadgets are text feeds. This is reflected in the rather nifty "Widget/Reader" switch.

- At the top of the screen, between the words "Widget" and "Reader" is a switch icon. By default your NetVibe homepage is set to display widgets.

- To change modes, click on the switch. Articles accessible within each widget are now compiled into one long list.

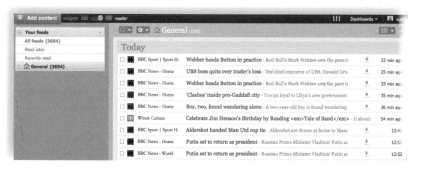

Additional portal sites

24eyes	http://www.24eyes.com	Itsastart	http://www.itsastart.com
Eskobo	http://www.eskobo.com	Klipfolio	http://www.serence.com
Favoor	http://www.favoor.com	Pageflakes	http://www.pageflakes.com
Feedtv	http://www.feedfeeds.com	Pobb	http://www.pobb.net
Googlemodules	http://www.googlemodules.com	Protopage	http://www.protopage.com
Gritwire	http://www.gritwire.com	Windowslive	http://www.live.com
Inbox	http://www.inbox.com	Wrickr	http://www.wrickr.com

Security Issues

Online commerce continues to expand at a rapid rate as we devote more time to activities that require us to make payments to a remote user, either using our credit cards or PayPal accounts. It's clear that criminals are increasingly taking advantage of carelessness or ignorance on the part of the consumer. Indeed, in 2011, the British government's Cabinet Office published estimates that cybercrime was costing the British economy the equivalent of $40 billion per year. Even though many other experts have questioned the arrival of such an extraordinary figure, it's nonetheless clear that Internet crime, and the problem of identity theft, is now a major issue. In this section we'll look at the subject of security, from the simple steps you can take when creating and storing passwords, to more complex solutions, such as Virtual Private Networks, which controls the potential for other parties to monitor your online activities.

Security Basics

A good deal of online crime is simply a result of lax password security. Most modern applications won't allow you to set up an obvious password, such as one of your names, your date of birth, or that great all-time security classic "password"! But cyber criminals are often clever people—and Internet users are sometimes foolish, gullable, or naïve. We've all had unsolicited e-mails purportedly from Nigerian princes or lawyers representing deceased billionaires telling us that we are now unexpectedly wealthy...so long as we hand over our banking details. (I had one just this morning from Mr. Ban Ki-moon, the Secretary-General of the United Nations, who had broken off his important work in the Middle East to tell me that I now had a US bank account worth $37.2 million...if I sent him some very specific personal information!) We can laugh about these e-mails and assume that nobody would be sufficiently idiotic to follow up on such irresistible offers, yet criminals surely wouldn't devote their time to "phishing" in this way if they were not getting the occasional taker.

Some criminals, however, are altogether more pernicious in their approach, sending out "Trojan" programs to gather information—these usually take the form of .exe files attached to spam e-mails—or "botnets" to infect PCs for use in viral attacks. Scarier still are so-called Man-in-the-Middle attacks, where a third party is able to intercept and sometimes modify e-mails without the knowledge of either the sender of receiver. These may be rare, but there are still steps you can take to protect your life online.

As the 2011 Sony Playstation Network fiasco illustrated, sometimes these matters are out of our control, and we just have to hope that those selling us online services have systems in place to protect our stored data from hacker attacks. (Stolen from Sony in April 2011 were personal details of 77 million users, including 2.2 million sets of credit card data.)

The Dos and Don'ts of Passwords

Most of us now require multiple passwords for our varied online activities, so as a starting point, let's look at some basic approaches to choosing a password. The two most important aspects here are security of access and, of course, memorability.

One password covers all Don't use the same password to cover all of your security needs. Fear of forgetting a password is an obvious concern for many. (Although most websites do have a pretty secure system in place for helping us out on those occasions when we do forget.) If you take this approach and someone *does* gain access to your password then you may find that your entire life has been compromised!

Develop an Algorithm One sensible approach is to take an aspect of the name of the website and then add a series of digits that only you know. One example may be to use the 5th, 4th, 3rd, and 2nd letter of the website along with last four digits of your best friend's telephone number. In this example, you might set up a Paypal password of **APYA3209**, and your Amazon password might be **OZAM3209**. This has the advantage of providing you with memorable yet different passwords for all of your different accounts. (When choosing a number, though, it's important that it can't obviously be tied to you. So don't use your own telephone number, for example.)

Focus on each letter Sometimes you will be assigned a password that you cannot change. One way to remember a randomized, assigned, difficult password is to take a mnemonic approach: think of a sentence where each word begins with the letter of your password. So, "ffhdn" could be remembered as "fish fingers have dirty nails." The more absurd the sentence, the easier you will be able to picture it in your mind.

Remove the vowels Take a memorable word or phrase and remove the vowels from it. For example, the phrase "**give me the fish**" creates a password of "**gvmthfsh**."

Use the keyboard layout This can be used on its own or, for added security, with one of the other techniques. If your password doesn't use the keys "1," "Q," "A," or "Z," take your chosen word (or previously generated password) and hit the key to the left of your password. So if your chosen word is "flute97" create a password of "dkyrw86." Obviously you can choose keys above, below, or to the right…just as long as you remember which!

Anagrams Take two words with the same number of letters and jumble them in a systematic manner. Thus if your two words were "**fish**" and "**chip**" you could alternate letters from each word to create a password of "**fcihsihp**."

Turn letters into numbers This idea uses the letters and numbers found on some telephone pads. Take two words that combine in a memorable way—for example "**trumpet**" and "**fish**"—and convert the letters to their respective numbers. The pasword here would be "**87867383474**."

Password Software
There are plenty of applications out there, either web-based or for installation on a desktop, that can help you either create, remember, or store your passwords. Let's look at a couple of examples.

Roboform

http://www.roboform.com

Introduced in 1999, Roboform is a password management and Internet form-filling program, which is installed on the computer desktop. Roboform offers an efficient solution to the problem of remembering multiple complex passwords for different websites. When installed, whenever you enter a password-protected website, Roboform will launch a pop-up dialogue

box asking if you would like to automate the process. If you agree, in the future you won't have to worry about this process—Roboform will do it on your behalf. There is only one password you need to remember, and that is the master pasword to the Roboform account.

Pixelock

http://www.pixelock.com

An interesting alternative approach to password management is offered by the Pixelock website, which uses an image recognition system. The user uploads an image of their own over which Pixelock places a grid. Instead of using words and numbers to create a password, the user clicks on a sequence of boxes from the grid. This can then be applied to any password-protected website.

Malware

An all-inclusive term, Malware covers such areas as spyware, adware, trojans, viruses, and other unpleasant or annoying types of software that can infect our computers. At best these can be annoying—the pop-up adware that usually advertises online gambling or pornography; at worst, some viruses can completely cripple your operating systems. Similarly, a trojan downloader can be used to trick the user into allowing the virus computer access, which then delivers/installs active malware components. Let's look at them in a little more detail.

Virus A small program that can enter a computer in a variety of different ways, often via e-mail attachments or portable devices such as flash drives. Some viruses have the ability to reproduce themselves automatically and infect as many files as possible. The impact of a virus may be devastating to a computer system.

Worm A worm is like a virus, its intention to infect networks, delete files, and open backdoors for other malicious programs.

Trojan Taking its name from the Trojan Horse of Greek mythology, this type of malware enters your computer system disguised as a harmless program—usually downloaded from the Internet—but when installed begins executing hidden, potentially destructive tasks, such as opening doors for other malware. A trojan can delete files, change settings, and begin installing other programs. Annoyingly, some trojans can also change antivirus setting to avoid detection of the malware it intends to install.

Spyware It's been estimated that 90% of computers are infected with some form of spyware. Spyware applications are installed on a computer with the aim of gathering information without the user's knowledge. This data is not necessarily used for any malicious purposes—mostly it will track shopping and browsing habits that might be collected and sent to third party organizations. (Ever wondered why, if you happen to spend an evening casually researching bicycles, you soon find yourself inundated with cycle-related browser ads?) Spyware is, however, capable of passing on more private information. Most spyware is installed along with free software downlaoded from the Internet.

Adware This kind of software exists to show you advertisements, pop-up windows and browser hijacking being the most common types. These are more annoying than malicious, but they can slow down your system.

Backdoor A program that enters your computer and creates an opening that may allow another user to take control of the computer system, which may then be used to carry out illegal actions.

Malware Protection

There is a wide variety of software available to identify and remove malware from a computer system—or even prevent it from getting on there in the first place. Having some kind of system in place is highly advisable, especially if you use a Windows-based PC (Mac users are not generally subjected to the same malware onslaught).

Bitdefender

http://www.bitdefender.com

A well-established name in the antivirus field, Bitdefender also offers the free web-based QuickScan diagnosis for Windows computers. Its premium AntiVirus+ package claims to remove viruses, spyware, and adware.

Virtual Private Networks

What we've looked at so far places basic security concerns in the hands of the user. But how secure or private is the data that passes from our computers or other devices? The truth is, we can never know. In theory, anyone from our Internet service provider (ISP) or the network we're connecting through, may be able to monitor our online activities. Some of this potential control comes from being able to track your IP address. This is a code allocated to you—either temporarily or permanently—by your ISP and, while in use, is unique to your computer. This information is also stored by some websites and search engines you may visit, and can be used by marketing organizations to target potential customers.

To avoid this happening you can use a virtual personal network (VPN), which generates a stealth IP address and makes it theoretically impossible for anyone—ISP, website, or search engine—to trace your *real* IP address. This can also enable you to use websites that have been regionalized: some American websites, for example, are only available to IP addresses logged within the United States.

VPNs are frequently used by businesses to bring the security of a private network to an insecure public network, especially necessary when its users are in remote locations. Some individuals also create VPNs in the belief that should they engage in illegal activities—such as filesharing—they will become more difficult to trace.

Virtual Private Networks perhaps require a greater level of technical ability, but it's possible to subscribe to commercial VPN services that provide software to download to your desktop for less than $10 per month.

VPN Sites		Anti-Malware Sites	
12VPN	https://12vpn.com	Avast! Pro	http://www.avast.com
Black Logic	https://www.blacklogic.com	Bitdefender	http://www.bitdefender.com
Express VPN	https://www.express-vpn.com	ChicaPC-Shield	http://www.chicalogic.com
Happy VPN	http://www.happy-vpn.com	ESET NOD32	http://ww.eset.co.uk
Hide My Ass	http://www.hidemyass.com/vpn	Kaspersky	http://www.kaspersky.com
Liberty VPN	http://www.liberty-vpn.info	Lavasoft Ad-Aware	http://www.lavasoft.com
Overplay	https://www.overplay.net	Malwarebytes	http://shop.malwarebytes.org
Strong VPN	http://strongvpn.com	Norton AntiVirus	http://www.norton.com
Swiss VPN	http://www.swissvpn.net	Super AntiSpyware	http://www.superantispyware.com
VyprVPN	https://www.goldenfrog.com	Webroot Antivirus	http://www.webroot.com

Search Engines

If there is a single type of web-based application that could be said to be at the heart of the Internet, it must be the search engine. Whether your favored search site is Yahoo!, Google, or any of the many other available possibilities, the basic concept is similar: you type in a keyword, string of text, or a Boolean search, and receive a list of websites that most closely contain your search criteria. You can then click on any of the items from that list to open the website.

Search History

The first application for searching on the Internet was a program called Archie that was created in 1990 at McGill University in Montreal, Canada. Archie downloaded directory listings located on anonymous FTP sites to create a searchable database of filenames. However, it could not read the contents of the files, so it depended on a logical naming structure being in place.

The first web search engine, Wandex, appeared in 1993. This compiled its information, like most subsequent engines, using a "web crawler"—an automated program that browses the web collecting data. The following year saw the launch of many of the most popular search engines of the 1990s, such as Lycos, Excite, Infoseek, Inktomi, Northern Light, Ask Jeeves, Yahoo!, and AltaVista. Indeed, it was commercial interest in these so-called first generation search engines that fueled much of the first Internet stock-market boom.

The second generation of search engines began to appear toward the end of decade, among them, in 1998, Google, the most popular search engine of them all. The success was based in part on the use of link analysis and the PageRank analysis algorithm—a numerical weighting system which helped to make searches more relevant and accurate. In fact, such search engines typically use more than 150 different criteria to determine relevancy.

The most recent developments in web searches have aimed to refine relevancy even further. We'll take a look at a selection of these toward the end of this segment of the book.

Google

http://www.google.com

Google is perhaps the most astonishing success story in the history of the Internet. It began in 1996 as a research project by Larry Page and Sergey Brin, two doctoral students at Stanford University in California. Their basic idea was that a search engine that analyzed the relationships between websites would produce better results than existing techniques, which largely ranked results according to the number of times the search term appeared on a page. The name "Google" originated from a misspelling of the term "googol," which refers to the number 1 followed by 100 zeros. The business was initially run from a friend's garage, but by 2010 Google employed over 25,000 full-time staff and had an estimated stock market value of $160 billion. Such is its ubiquity that in 2006 the term "to google" was given its own entry in the Oxford English Dictionary. In May 2011, Google broke a new record having achieved over one billion unique visitors for the first time

Simple Search

• Begin by entering Google's URL: **http://www.google. com**. (If you are outside the United States, you might find yourself automatically transferred to one of Google's local sites—shown here, the UK version.) One of the reasons Google was instantly popular was because it was so simple to use. All you have to do is type in some text and click on the **Search** button. In

this example we will enter the word **Fish**. As you enter each letter, Google will begin and gradually refine its search.

• You will see a list of what Google considers to be the 10 most relevant websites that match your search criteria. If you want to see the next 10 ranked websites, then click on the button marked **2** at the foot of the page. You continue to view more search results by clicking on the subsequent numbers.

Alternative Searches

When you launch Google, it immediately assumes that you want to do a web search—and this is what the vast majority of users do want. However, above the search box you see further options: besides Web, you can search for **Images**, **Videos**, **Maps**, and **News**. And if you click on **More**, then you will see a whole new page of options.

• Let's use our existing search text to look for images. With the word "**Fish**" still in the search box, click on **Images**.

• Google now provides you with a page of thumbnail views of websites that it believes match your search requirements.

• To get a full-size view of any of the websites shown on the page, you simply click on the image.

• If you click on the X in the top right-hand corner of the image, that window will close, leaving in place the website on which it appears.

Search Criteria

Doing a search is very straightforward—you simply enter a word and click on the **Search** button. There is a bit of skill involved in choosing the correct terms, though. Here is a brief guide:

Choose your words with care Start with the obvious. If you want general information about, say, London, try typing in **London**! If you want to find a place in London to rent a car, try **London car hire**. Google, like most search engines, is not case sensitive, so if you enter **London, london, LONDON,** or **lOnDoN,** it will generate the same results.

Exclude common words If you are searching on multiple criteria, there is no need to include "and" between terms. Also, many search engines ignore common terms, such as "how" and "where," as well as certain single digits and letters. Google will tell you if it has omitted a common word. If your search critically requires this word to be included, you can place a "+" sign in front of it.

Exact phrases Sometimes you will want to search for a very specific phrase—for example, a line from poem or a person's name. To do this, place quotation marks around your search term. So if you want to do a web search for Tony Blair, enter "Tony Blair"—otherwise you may find options that list the words "Tony" and "Blair."

Negatives Some words have multiple meanings. You can use the "minus" sign to filter unwanted items. For example, bass might refer to a fish or a musical instrument. If your intended search is the latter, you could enter bass -fish. This should avoid any fish-related sites being selected.

Even More Google

If you click on the **More** button at the top of the toolbar, you will find further search options and other Google tools. At the bottom of the drop-down menu, click on Even More. This opens a new window that details around 30 other Google applications that can be accessed. Among them is **Books**, which takes you to an index of titles that can be read in full on your browser.

Search Engines: The New Wave

The past five years have seen a number of new developments in the world of the search engine, many driven by what used to be called "Web 2.0" technologies, such as AJAX. They don't represent a radical overhaul of the commercial big guns, such as Google, Bing, and Ask, but rather an enhancement—and anything particularly noteworthy will doubtless be subsumed by the industry leaders in the future.

Yippy

http://www.yippy.com

Formerly known as Clusty, Yippy is a "clustering" engine that groups similar items together and organizes search results into "clouds" or folders. Yippy is a "meta-search" system, so it searches other search engines. The categorization makes for a neater and more refined search experience. So if you're looking for a specific subject, you are likely to get the best results by navigating the categories and their subdivisions.

Blekko

http://www.blekko.com

An interesting newcomer, Blekko was founded in 2007 by Rich Skrenta and funded in part by Netscape entrepreneur Marc Andreesen, with the aim of producing purer searches than could be achieved with Google. The site launched successfully at the end of 2010 and is already one of the top-ten global search engines. Blekko has established itself as the "slashtag" search tool. A slashtag is a user-defined search engine that aims to filter out spam or content farms, and thus—in theory, at least—list only relevant, content-strong sites.

Rollyo

http://www.rollyo.com

This is a community-powered, theme-based search. Rollyo allows users to create and publish their own personal search engines. This is achieved by creating custom "SearchRolls" made up of URLs that the user knows to be useful in a specific category. This means that while it's not as exhaustive as a traditional search engine, you get results based on the recommendations of real people, rather than a mathematical algorithm.

Swicki

http://www.eurekster.com

Like Rollyo, Swicki is a social networking search engine that allows users to create focused searches based on the input of other Swicki users.

More Search Engines

Blogpulse	http://www.blogpulse.com	Omgili	http://www.omgili.com
Exalead	http://www.exalead.com	Quintura	http://qelix.com
Factbites	http://www.factbites.com	Surfwax	http://www.surfwax.com
Gahooyoogle	http://www.gahooyoogle.com	Technorati	http://www.technorati.com
Hakia	http://www.hakia.com	Wikimatrix	http://www.wikimatrix.org
Healthline	http://www.healthline.com	Wink	http://wink.com
Icerocket	http://www.icerocket.com	Yoono	http://www.yoono.com
Lexxe	http://www.lexxe.com	Yubnub	http://www.yubnub.org
Liveplasma	http://www.liveplasma.com		
Makidi	http://www.makidi.com		
Nextaris	http://www.nextaris.com		
Prase us	http://www.prase.us		
Prefound	http://www.prefound.com		
Releton	http://www.releton.com		

Social Networking

In its brief life, the Internet has been responsible for introducing the world to a wide array of buzzwords. Most of these terms have emanated from the technical, scientific, and academic communities, disseminated through the media, before merging into the mainstream and eventually becoming

unutterable clichés. One recent addition to this canon is the term "social networking"—the practice of expanding social contacts by making connections through others. It's rather like the concept of "six degrees of separation," the idea that it would be possible for any two people on the planet to make contact through a chain of no more than five intermediaries. In a similar way, social networking on the Internet enables people to make new and relevant contacts with those they would have been unlikely to have otherwise met. In the time since the first edition of this book was published, this area has seen dramatic change. Back in 2007, MySpace was the clear brand leader, Facebook was noted for its growing popularity, and Twitter barely elicited a mention. Facebook is now the second most heavily used website in the world, and Twitter has been credited/blamed for everything from the Arab Spring activities in North Africa and the Middle East to the 2011 London riots. And MySpace has rather fallen from grace.

Background to Social Networking Sites

It's fair to say that social networking of some sort has been taking place almost as long as societies themselves have existed. However, the number of people who now have access to the Internet means that what once would had to have taken place face-to-face in a fixed location can now occur between two computer screens anywhere in the world.

Unsurprisingly, social networking was one of the earliest types of website to achieve popularity. One of the first to be launched was Classmates.com, which began in 1995. Like many others that followed, it existed primarily as a way of keeping old school and college friends in touch with one another. Inspired by its popularity, Friends Reunited enjoyed similar success in Europe when it launched four years later. Others sites emerged, usually with a target audience in mind. MySpace, for example, was initially only really attractive to teenagers; Facebook was aimed at university students. However, all have had to evolve as their users have grown up, and most are now globally inclusive.

Estimates of the numbers of people actively engaged in social networking make for some fascinating reading. A survey in 2011 estaimated that an incredible 47% of American adults use a social networking website—for the vast majority of those users, Facebook is the site of choice.

Facebook

http://www.facebook.com

Back in 2007, in the first edition of this book, I wrote, "MySpace is the most stunning phenomenon of the new Internet era." Fast-forward only a couple years, and MySpace had already become passé as we all turned to Facebook for our social networking needs. So let me start again.

As modern-day Internet success stories go, Facebook represents the most stunning of examples. Launched in 2004, it was created by Harvard University student Mark Zuckerberg and two of his roommates. The project started as a computer game but gradually evolved into an online social networking utility for the use of other Harvard students. Such was its success that within a few weeks over half of the undergraduates on campus are said to have registered. Facebook quickly expanded, first inviting students from other Ivy League colleges, then opening it up to all students, and then the rest of the world.

Following this immediate success, advertising revenue rose at such a dramatic rate that Zuckerberg left Harvard to run Facebook full time. He has since turned down a number of multimillion dollar takeover deals.

To call Facebook ubiquitous is to understate the impact it has had on the way people communicate and interact. It is now second only to Google in terms of global Internet traffic, so widely used that it frequently makes headline news whenever it undergoes one of its periodic updates. Hollywood considered the Facebook story so irresistible that it was retold in the 2010 film *The Social Network*. And founder Mark Zuckerberg is now so well known that his every utterance on the future of technology is reported by the press.

Why Facebook?

The idea behind Facebook is simple: a network of individuals posts comments, photographs, videos, and links, and responds to the same types of material posted by others in the network. It isn't in itself particularly radical, in essence doing little more than MySpace or Bebo had done several years before, so its incredible success is perhaps a little difficult to fathom. One initial appeal was its simplicity of use and rather sober look—a stark contrast to the brash colors and confusing muddle of the design that was MySpace. In turn, this also helped create the impression that its target demographic was not high school students. There was, perhaps, also an element of snob appeal—Facebook started life as an Ivy League project, an association that appealed to many who joined the first wave of expansion. Whatever the reason, Facebook became fashionable, and thereafter buried itself deeply into the everday lives of its users. It's now the first point of online communication for a significant proportion of its users—traditional e-mail systems often having been replaced by Facebook messages. So, if you have somehow avoided social networking sites up until now, why should you use Facebook? The most obvious answer is probably because all of your friends and collagues are already on there.

Getting Started with Facebook

Let's now set up a Facebook account and take a look at some of the features offered.

• Enter the URL: **http://www.facebook.com**.

• Facebook will now ask for some basic registration information, such as name, e-mail address, password, gender, and date of birth. Enter these details and click on **Sign Up**.

• For security purposes, respond to the "captcha" by typing in the two words and clicking on the **Sign Up** button.

• The first step of the set-up process appears. This window enables you to find friends using your e-mail systems. We'll leave this for now. Click on the **Ignore** button.

• Step 2 enables you to enter optional education and employment details. Click on **Save & Continue**.

• Step 3 is where you can add a profile photograph. You can either browse your desktop for an image or use a connected

webcam. When the photograph has been uploaded, click on **Save & Continue**.

• Facebook will now send an e-mail to your account. Click on the link in the e-mail to complete the sign-up process. Your very basic Facebook account has now been created.

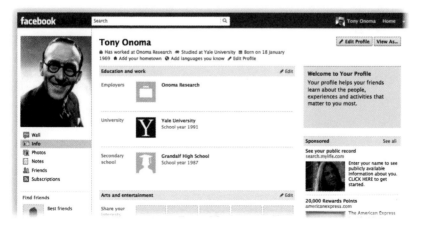

Finding Facebook Friends

Without friends, the Facebook experience, like any other social networking site, would be a useless one. Facebook offers a number of simple ways of finding out if people who you already know are on Facebook. One method is

to enable Facebook to look into your e-mail account and match addresses of your contacts against those of other Facebook users. Let's look at an example of tracing possible friends using a Windows Live Hotmail account. (You can also use your Yahoo!, Skype, BT, and AOL accounts in a similar manner.)

• From your Facebook homepage, click on the **Friends** tab on the left of the screen.

• In the Windows Live Hotmail box, enter your Hotmail address and click on **Find Friends**.

• In this case one possible friend has been discovered among your Hotmail contacts. If you know this person and want also to make him a Facebook contact, click on the **Add Friends** button.

• Facebook now sends a friend request to this person. They will decide whether or not they want you to be a friend.

• If the other person agrees, you will receive a notification from Facebook. Whenever you receive a notification, it will be indicated in the menu bar as a number positioned alongside the globe icon. (The number tells you how many notifications you have.)

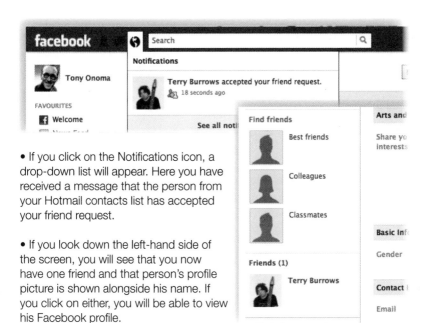

• If you click on the Notifications icon, a drop-down list will appear. Here you have received a message that the person from your Hotmail contacts list has accepted your friend request.

• If you look down the left-hand side of the screen, you will see that you now have one friend and that person's profile picture is shown alongside his name. If you click on either, you will be able to view his Facebook profile.

Receiving Facebook Friend Requests

Let's now look at what happens when somebody asks you to be their Facebook friend.

• On the menu bar alongside the Facebook logo, you will see a "people" icon—this is the **Friends** button. If you see a number alongside it, you can tell that you have a friend request from another Facebook user. Click on the button.

• You can see the identity of the person asking to be your friend. To approve the request, click on the **Confirm** button. A new button will appear labeled **Add To List**. If you want to add this person to your list of Facebook friends, click on the button.

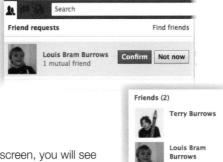

• If you look down the left of the screen, you will see that you now have two friends.

Sending Facebook Messages

There are two seemingly distinct methods of sending messages in Facebook.
One relies on both parties being online at the same time; the other does not.

• In the menu bar, click on the
Message tab. From the pop-up
window, click on **Send a New
Message**.

• In the New Message
window, select the recipient
of your message. Each
additional letter you type in
the **To** box refines a list of

possibilities from your list
of friends. This can save a
good deal of time if you have
hundreds of contacts. Click
on the name.

• Type in your message
and then click on the Send button. You will receive a brief notification that the
message has been successfully sent.

Facebook Chat

If two users are online at the same time, Facebook allows for instant messaging.
You can see at a glance how many of your Facebook friends are also online by
looking at the **Chat** panel on the bottom right-hand corner of the window—

indicated by the number in brackets. In this
example, the number "1" is displayed.

• Click on the **Chat** panel and it will open out
to display the names of
those online. To chat,
click on the name. An
individual chat window
will open.

• Type your message
in the bottom of the
panel and press send to
transmit. The messages
are displayed above.

Although these are two different forms of message, they are stored the same way.

• Click on the **Message** icon and then **See All Messages**.

• You will see that both types of message are displayed as part of the same sequence.

Facebook Status Updates

At the very heart of Facebook's social networking functions are status updates. These may be messages, photographs, videos, or other links that are published on the user's homepage—or "Wall"—and that appear in the newsfeeds circulated to everyone within the network. Here's where a good deal of Facebook's activity takes place.

• Click on the **Wall** button from the list on the left of the screen.

• In the **Update Status** box you can begin typing your message.

• The two icons on the bottom left of the box enable you to show other Facebook friends you are with and your location. Click on either button to enter details.

• When you have finished your entry, click on **Post**. (Think for a few moments before you do this—many a Facebook user has regretted a hasty status update!)

• On the left is a newsfeed from one of your friends' Facebook homepages. This is how your posting will appear to the outside world.

Google+

https://plus.google.com

When the world's biggest Internet presence decides to muscle in on the social networking scene, then there's every possibility that it might succeed dramatically. Only launched in trial mode in the summer of 2011, Google announced that there are over 10 million users registered within the first two weeks. Time will tell whether Google + has anything fundamentally different to woo Facebook users.

Sense and Safety

At its purest and least commercial, social networking is all about self-expression as well as connecting with and making friends. However, you should remember that you are, in effect, speaking to the world and what you post publicly could later come back to haunt you or expose you to danger. Here are some commonsense guidelines that you should follow when using any social networking site.

Public space Your profile is a public space, so don't post anything you wouldn't want the world to know, such as your address or telephone number. Above all, avoid posting information that could make it easy for a stranger to find you.

Embarrassment Think twice before posting a photo or making public comments. Can you think of *anyone* who you might not want to view your online behavior? Your family? Your friends? Your boss?

Appropriate content Harassment, bullying, hate mail, and other inappropriate content should always be reported to site authorities.

Beware of strangers Take care when adding strangers as friends—people aren't always who they claim to be. Think VERY carefully before agreeing to meet someone in person whom you have met in this way. If you *must* meet someone, do it in a public place and take a friend along with you.

Scams Be on the lookout for fraudulent activities like "phishing"—a method used by criminals to try to get personal information by pretending to be a familiar site. Remember the golden rule of online common sense: if someone makes you an offer that looks too good to be true, then it probably *is* too good to be true.

MySpace

http://www.myspace.com

One of the first major successes of the Internet, MySpace was founded in 2003 by Tom Anderson, Chris DeWolfe, and a small group of programmers. For the first three years of its existence, MySpace was simply *the* social network site, introducing the concept to the vast majority of its users, who found the personal profiles, "friend" networks, and high-quality media content hard to resist—at least until Facebook

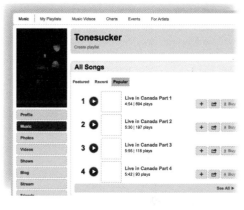

stole its thunder. Success brought very swift rewards: in 2005 the company was bought out for $580 million by Rupert Murdoch's News Corporation.

While the network communication side of MySpace's business has been all but demolished by the success of Facebook, it remains a popular forum for discovering new music. Indeed, setting up a MySpace page with added music, photographs and videos is generally viewed as an essential part of creating a new band.

Bebo

http://www.bebo.com

Launched in 2005, for a time Bebo was almost as widely used as MySpace and Facebook. Operating in much the same way as the other major social networking sites, Bebo's initial user base was more likely to be teenagers. Bought out by AOL in 2008 for $850 million—a figure most observers saw

as vastly overvalued—the site almost came to a premature end in 2010 when AOL, unwilling to make the necessary investment to compete with Facebook, announced plans to close Bebo down altogether. It was eventually sold on to a capital investment group for a sum reputed to be less than $10 million.

Twitter

http://www.twitter.com

Described as the "SMS of the Internet," Twitter is an online social networking and microblogging system. It was created in 2006 by Jack Dorsey and rapidly gained worldwide popularity. As of 2011 there are an estimated 200 million users generating over 200 million messages and handling over 1.6 billion search queries.

Part of its appeal is in its simplicity. Communication is mainly through public messages—broadly equivalent to Facebook status updates—that enable its users to send and read posts limited in length to 140 characters. These are widely known as "tweets." The user can "follow" other Twitter users or be followed. Any tweets from those you follow will be visible on your Twitter homepage.

It's also possible to perform keyword searches—useful for following trending subjects. This gives access to *all* tweets, not only those posted by those you follow.

Twitter has been credited with helping to enable communication under repressive regimes. There are critics, however, and some have characterized Twitter as being part of an "addiction to constant self-affirmation".

Using Twitter

Let's now set up a new Twitter account and look at how to perform the basic operations.

• Begin by entering the URL: **http://www.twitter. com**. On the front page you will see an area headed "New to Twitter?". Enter your name, e-mail address, and a password. Click on the **Sign Up** button.

• On a second screen, Twitter allocates you an available user name. If you don't like this, you can enter something different, although it must be unique, so Twitter will check whether it's already in use before you go any further. Click on **Create My Account** when you have finished.

• Carry on with the registration process by entering the "captcha" in the box provided, and then clicking on the button labeled **Continue to My Account**.

• Twitter starts off by giving you a handful of celebrity names to follow. You can also search for other celebrities stored in different categories. Here we've selected **Technology**, which gives us, among others, the option of following the tweets of Steve Case, one of the founders of AOL. Click on the **Next Step: Friends** button.

• Like Facebook, Twitter will let you use the most popular e-mail systems to find new contacts to follow. Here we'll click on the **Hotmail** button.

• Enter your Hotmail address and password and click on **Connect**.

• The Hotmail search yields one successful result. If you want to become a "follower" of this person's tweets, click on the **Follow** button. (If the search had turned up more than one contact, you could have clicked on the **Follow All** button.) Click on the **Finish** button.

You will now be sent an e-mail by Twitter. Click on the link to verify your account. You can now use all of Twitter's features. If you click on the **Home** button on the menu, you will see that almost all of the current tweets are from the person you found in your Hotmail search.

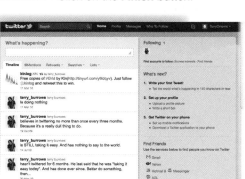

Updating Your Twitter Profile

You can personalize your Twitter account by adding photographs and some descriptive information. To access your current details, click on the **Profile** tab in the main menu.

• Click on **Edit Your Profile**. This takes you to the **Settings** page.

• The **Settings** page has a number of different tabs where you can change details such as passwords and layout. Click on the **Profile** tab.

• You can add a photograph (by browsing through your hard drive) or alter your real name (your user name is now fixed), location, home website, and biography. Click on **Save** when you are finished.

• If you now click on the **Profile** tab at the top of the screen you will see how your changes look. This is your Twitter public profile.

Tony Onoma
@TonyOnoma New York City
Musician. Writer. Any resemblance to the old English comedian Arthur Askey is purely coincidental!
http://www.tonyonoma.com

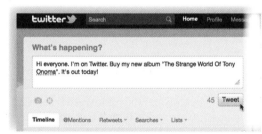

Your First Tweet

Posting a tweet is extremely simple. You must first be logged in. If you're not already there, click on the **Home** tab on your homepage. At the top of the screen you will see a message "What's happening?"—enter your message in the box below. Unlike Facebook and other social networks, where status updates can be several paragraphs long, Twitter restricts you to 140 characters. (You will quickly see that there is an art to coming up with succinct postings that fit in with this limitation.) The number beneath the box indicates how many characters you have left. When you are ready, click on the **Tweet** button.

Twitter Search

You can find out what's going on in the "Twittersphere" by doing a keyword search on a subject of interest.

• In the search box found in the menu bar, enter your text and click on **Enter**. In this case we'll do a search for tweets relating to soccer star David Beckham.

• On the left of the window you will see a list of tweets relating to your keyword search. On the right of the screen you will find Tweeters that match your search.

• If you highlight one of the individual tweets, it will appear in full on the right of the screen. Any highlighted tweet gives you the option of "retweeting"—sending it to all of your followers—or replying directly to the tweet. (The individual buttons are shown beneath the message.)

Tips For Tweeters

Tweet often Try to keep our audience hooked
Add links to your website Try to drive traffic through to your site
Include your feed Include the link to your Twitter feed in all your communications
Use hastags Hashtags (# tags) are used for adding metadata to your tweets
Ask questions Try to get a response from your followers by posing questions
Retweet Increase circulation by asking your followers to pass on your tweets

43 Things

http://www.43things.com

43 Things is a social networking site that uses "tagging" principles to link people together. Users create accounts and then make a list of their hopes, goals, or dreams. These are then connected with users who have created lists with similarly worded ideas. 43 Things was created by the Robot Co-op using the Ruby On Rails programming language and officially launched in 2005. In its first year, it won a Webby Award as best social networking site, and a year later it had reached the landmark of having over one million registered users.

• Enter the URL: **http://www.43things.com**. Go through the registration process and sign in.

• The main 43 Things page contains a "cloud" of tags based on information entered by other users. Like most clouds, tags that have a greater number of entries attached to them are shown more prominently. You can browse the cloud and click on any individual entry, or you can make your own entry. Let's do the latter, and create a goal to swim the English Channel.

• Look for the box beneath the question: "What do you want to do with your life?" Enter **Swim the English Channel**. Click on the button marked **I Want to Do This**.

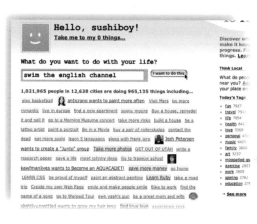

• The results screen will appear. As you can see, in this example there are 58 users who have swimming the English Channel as one of their goals. The top half of the screen lists the 10 most recent people to list the same goal. If you scroll to the bottom of the list, you can see if any of the users sharing this goal have posted comments.

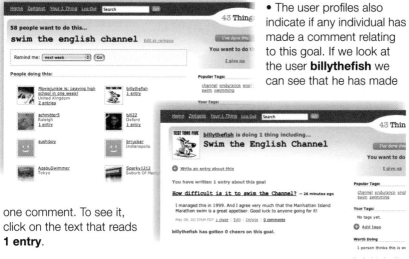

• The user profiles also indicate if any individual has made a comment relating to this goal. If we look at the user **billythefish** we can see that he has made

one comment. To see it, click on the text that reads **1 entry**.

We can see that this user claims to have already swum the English Channel. What's more, he also offers what seems to be good advice on how to do it. And this is the essence of 43 Things—if you have a goal in mind, getting help from someone who has already been there can only be a good thing.

Linkedin

http://www.linkedin.com

Linkedin is a social networking site aimed primarily at business professionals. Launched in 2005 by a group of former PayPal employees, five years later *Silicon Valley Insider* ranked it among the top ten most valuable start-ups: by early 2011 the company was valued at over one-and-a-half million dollars. Reflecting a rather more sober and serious approach than other social networks, Linkedin also contains facilities for the formation of specialist professional groups and a popular job-listing feature.

Social Network Curiosities

Most of the networks we have looked at so far have been very generalized in terms of interest. There are, however, many strange and wonderful networks devoted to all types of niche groups. Here are a few.

Stache Passions

http://www.stachepassions.com

Like moustaches? Like people who sport moustaches? Want to be part of network of people that do? Stache Passions is indoubtedly the place for you!

Match A Dream

http://www.matchadream.com

This is the perfect site for anyone interested in dreams and their interpretation. Match A Dream allows users to record and share their dreams and others in the network to comment.

SocialGo

http://www.socialgo.com

Of course, if you can't find a social networking site that matches your interests you can always set one up of your own. There are a number of different sites that offer this service, among them SocialGo. It's very easy to use.

• Begin by entering the URL—**http:// www.socialgo.com**—and go through the registration process.

• In the first part of the setup page, enter the name of your network, a description, and its URL—in this case, **http://wwguitar-crazy.socialgo.com**.

2. Network design

• Scroll down the page to see the second part of the setup screen. This lets you design the look of your site. Click on any of the themes to see an expanded window. When you've made your choice, click on the **Continue** button.

• This takes you to your complete page. You can now send out invites with the URL to prospective members.

• To join the network, new members click on the **Sign Up** button.

Social Networking Websites

43places	http://www.43places.com	Meetup	http://www.meetup.com
Blogtronix	http://www.blogtronix.com	Mologogo	http://www.mologogo.com
Communitywalk	http://www.communitywalk.com	Mozes	http://mozes.com
		Myprogs	http://myprogs.net
		OpenBC	http://www.openbc.com
		Opinity	http://www.opinity.com
		Orkut	https://www.orkut.com
		Partysync	http://group.partysync.com
		Peerprofile	http://www.peerprofile.com
		Peertrainer	http://www.peertrainer.com
Friendster	http://www.friendster.com	Piczo	http://piczo.com
Gaia	http://hubs.gaia.com	Phusebox	http://phusebox.net
Giftbox	http://www.giftboxhome.com	Plum	http://www.plum.com
Greedyme	http://www.greedyme.com	Rabble	http://www.rabble.com
Groups	http://grou.ps	TheBlackStripe	http://www.theblackstripe.com
Ikarma	http://ikarma.com	Towncrossing	http://towncrossing.com
Linkedin	http://www.linkedin.com	Vcarious	http://www.vcarious.com
LiveJournal	http://www.livejournal.com	Ziggs	http://www.ziggs.com
Lovento	http://www.lovento.com		

Web-Based Office Software

The world of technology frequently throws up unexpected quirks on an unsuspecting world. Who, for example, would have imagined that SMS messaging—developed primarily for business users—would have been seized by teenagers and used to create a new type of language? However, one development that now seems highly predictable is the gradual and continued migration of software from the desktop to the Web. Products such as ThinkFree and Zoho were early movers in this field, giving a clear indication of how things would more than likely develop. Finally, in June 2011, after years of circulating rumors, Microsoft launched its web-based version of Office, the world's most widely used "productivity suite."

Microsoft Office 365

http://www.microsoft.com/office365

This now has to be the starting point for any discussion of web-based applications. But since Office 365 charges users a monthly subscription—which can cost as little as $6 per month for a basic package or $24 for the full works—we won't look at it in detail, when there are several free alternatives out there. Office 365 includes web-based versions of Outlook, Microsoft's e-mail reader; Word (*see below*); PowerPoint presentation tool (*see below*); the Excel spreadsheet (*see right*); and OneNote, the notetaking program (*see right*).

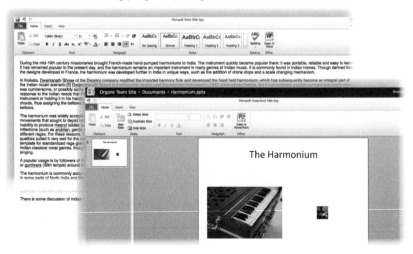

ThinkFree

http://www.thinkfree.com

During the time before Microsoft made its own web-based applications there was no shortage of bold new startups looking to fill this hole in the marketplace. Among the most prominent is ThinkFree.

Webtop Word Processing

ThinkFree is a suite of "webtop" office applications—word processor, spreadsheet, and presentation—each of which bears more than a passing resemblance to its Microsoft counterpart: each of these applications, in fact, is capable of reading and writing the relevant Microsoft file formats, so the clear aim here is to achieve universal compatibility.

Let's now take a look at ThinkFree's word processing capabilities.

• Begin by enter the URL: **http://www.thinkfree.com**. Before you can use ThinkFree you must first go through the registration process. Click on the button labeled **Sign On** in the top right-hand corner and follow the instructions. When you have finished, use your ID and password to log in.

• Click on the button marked **ThinkFree Online** in the menu bar at the top of the screen.

• Your **MyOffice** page will now open. To begin word processing, click on the blue **New Document** button.

(You'll notice that ThinkFree has even helpfully used the same colors as its Microsoft counterpart!)

• The **Create a New Document** window opens up. In the **File Name** box, you can give your document a title. You can now choose between **Quick Edit** or **Power Edit**: the former produces a simple text file; the latter is used for Microsoft Word format. Click on the **Power Edit** button and then on **Create a New Document**.

• An empty word processing document will appear in the screen that follows. You will notice that it contains the same principal features as most other word processors.

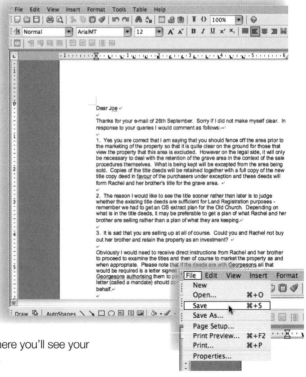

• Type in your text, and when you've finished, choose **Save** from the **File** menu. You will be returned to your own **MyOffice** page where you'll see your document in place.

Zoho

http://www.zoho.com

Zoho claims to be the world's first AJAX-based suite of web-based office programs. It's certainly wide-ranging in its scope, including takes on the most popular types of office software. For example: Zoho Writer is a word processor; Zoho Sheet is a spreadsheet system; Zoho Show is a presentation program; Zoho Projects and Zoho Planner are

project management tools; and Zoho Chat is an instant messenger. Most of these tools are capable of successfully importing and exporting the most widely used file formats.

Let's begin with a look at Zoho's spreadsheet program and how it can be used to import an existing standard Microsoft Excel file.

Zoho Sheet

Enter the URL: **http://www.zoho.com**. To use any of the Zoho applications, you must first register and then log in. You can also use your Facebook, Google, or Yahoo! IDs to do this.

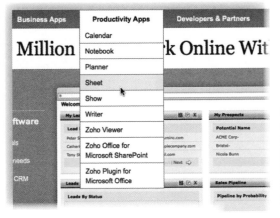

• We want to use the spreadsheet software, so begin by choosing **Productivity Apps** from the menu bar and **Sheet** from the drop-down menu.

197

• An empty spreadsheet will open. To begin importing an existing document, click on the **File** menu and from the drop-down menu choose **Import**. Two further options pop up: to load an existing Excel file, click on **Import File**.

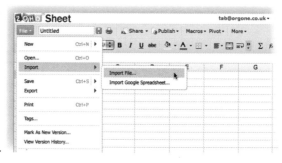

The import window opens. This lists the formats and file sizes supported by Zoho Sheets. Make sure that the Local File button is ticked and then click on the **Browse** button. Navigate through the folders on your hard drive until you find the desired Excel-format file.

When you click on the **Open** button, you will see that the name of the file you chose appears in the import window. Click on the **Import** button. The Excel document will now open. (If you want to load a spreadsheet from an online source, instead of clicking on the **Local File** button, chose **URL**, enter the web address and then **Import**.)

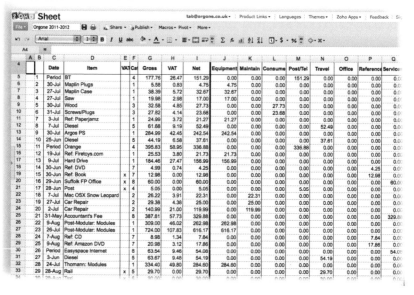

Share Your Sheet

You can let others either read or modify your spreadsheert. Click on **Share** and, from the drop-down menu, choose **Invite**. A new window will appear, enabling you to specify those with editorial permission. When you have finished, click on the **Share** button.

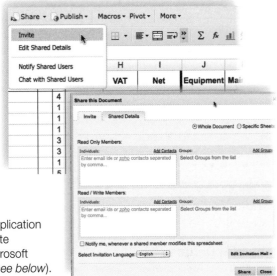

Zoho Show

Using the presentation application Zoho Show, you can create slide shows or import Microsoft PowerPoint documents (*see below*).

Zoho Writer

The Zoho suite also incorporates a word processing application called Writer. This operates in a very similar fashion to Microsoft Word and can import and export files in that format (*see below*).

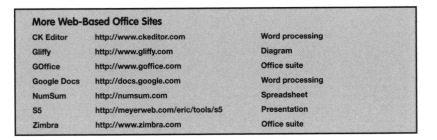

More Web-Based Office Sites

CK Editor	http://www.ckeditor.com	Word processing
Gliffy	http://www.gliffy.com	Diagram
GOffice	http://www.goffice.com	Office suite
Google Docs	http://docs.google.com	Word processing
NumSum	http://numsum.com	Spreadsheet
S5	http://meyerweb.com/eric/tools/s5	Presentation
Zimbra	http://www.zimbra.com	Office suite

Wikis and Collaboration

The notion of an application having its worth enhanced by the more people that use it is completely central to the whole concept of social networking. We've already seen a few collaborative applications at work—for example, online project diaries or calendars that can be updated by different members of a group. A "wiki" works in a similar way. It is a website that allows its users to add, change, or delete content within its pages. The term is used to describe collaborative authoring applications, of which the most famous (or infamous, perhaps) is Wikipedia. The word wiki comes from the Hawaiian language, where it means "quick," so any such application will enable its content to be accessed swiftly and simply.

The Wiki Debate

The idea of collaborative writing is an interesting one. A person can place an article on a wiki website; another can edit or rewrite it; and a third person can, if they choose, delete it altogether. So what are wikis good for? Certainly it's possible to set up a wiki webpage far more quickly than by using a dedicated web design program. And, once set up, wikis are very easy to maintain. Their collaborative potential is extremely good for brainstorming, compiling notes from a conference, meeting, or event, or preparing a document with others who are in different locations. However, there are potential pitfalls: if a wiki's content is open to all, then we can (and arguably should) have little or no control over those who may later edit the work. It is this very fact that has made Wikipedia—the world's largest online encyclopedia—such a controversial subject. Whereas most of us would expect contributors to anything claiming to be an encyclopedia to have some kind of expert credentials, absolutely *anyone* can write or edit a Wikipedia article. Thus, a fundamental criticism of Wikipedia is that its accuracy must *always* be in question and so would certainly not be suitable as a primary source of reference—at least without some kind of cross-checking. Another concern is that they may include a lack of neutrality normally expected from an encyclopedia and that some contributors may be working with some kind of hidden agenda. And there is the issue of emphasis: a popular athlete or actor might have a more detailed biography than a world leader.

In spite of such criticisms, in 2006 *Nature* magazine did a comparative study of science articles found on Wikipedia and their equivalents within *Encyclopaedia Britannica*. It found both to be similarly accurate. Some who have argued in favor of the wiki approach claim that any errors made on Wikipedia tend to be corrected quite quickly, so articles gradually become refined over time. Nevertheless, the fact still remains that, in the short term at least, you or I can go onto Wikipedia any time we choose and rewrite absolutely any piece of information—no matter how wrong, absurd, or defamatory it may be.

Wikipedia

http://www.wikipedia.org

The most important collaborative text application on the Internet, Wikipedia was first launched in 2001. It is run by the Wikipedia Foundation—a nonprofit organization set up by cofounder Jimmy Wales. As of July 2011, the encyclopedia held over 19 million articles written by over 90,000 active contributors. There are now editions of Wikipedia in 282 languages. Far and away the most popular general reference website on the Internet, it has long enjoyed a permanent place in the top 10 trafficked websites across the globe.

Searching for an Article

Wikipedia is extremely straightforward to use and usually provides swift results.

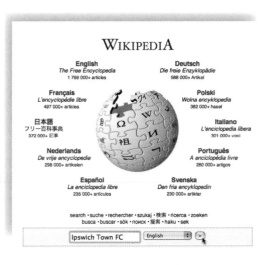

• Enter the URL: **http://www.wikipedia.org**. Enter a keyword for your search in the box on the main page. Wikipedia is available in many different local language versions, so select English from the drop-down list. Click on the arrow button (**>**).

• You will either see the article you have requested or, if there is more than one that matches your search text, what Wikipedia refers to as a "disambiguation list." This is a list containing a number of possible results. Click on any item in the list to open the article.

Editing an Article

Now let's look at how to make changes to an article on Wikipedia. Before going any further, decide whether or not you wish to register. It *is* possible to edit anonymously, but you should be aware that your IP address (the unique address of your computer connection to the Internet) will be logged, so your identity could, if necessary, be established without too much difficulty.

Let's make a change to the page we already have open.

• At the top of the window, click on the tab marked **Edit This Page**.

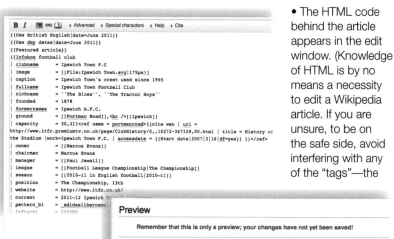

• The HTML code behind the article appears in the edit window. (Knowledge of HTML is by no means a necessity to edit a Wikipedia article. If you are unsure, to be on the safe side, avoid interfering with any of the "tags"—the

commands found within the arrowed brackets.) You can now edit your text.

• To see what your edit will look like, click on the button marked **Show Preview**.

• If you wish to put your changes "live," click on the button marked **Save Page**.

Preview

Remember that this is only a preview; your changes have not yet been saved!

Ipswich Town Football Club (◀ /ˈɪpswɪtʃ ˈtaʊn/; also known as **Ipswich**, **The Blues**, **Town**, or **The Tractor Boys**) are an English professional football team based in Ipswich, Suffolk. As of 2011, they play in the Football League Championship, having last appeared in the Premier League in 2001–02.

The club was founded in 1878 but did not turn professional until 1936, and was subsequently elected to join the Football League in 1938. They play their home games at Portman Road in Ipswich. The only fully professional football club in Suffolk, they have a long-standing and fierce rivalry with Norwich City in Norfolk, with whom they have contested the East Anglian derby 138 times since 1902.[2]

Ipswich won the English league title once, in 1961–62, and have been runners-up twice in 1980–81 and 1981–82. They won the FA Cup in 1977–78, and the UEFA Cup in 1980–81.

Content that violates any copyright will be deleted. Encyclopedic content must be **verifiable**. You agre

Edit summary (Briefly describe the changes you have made) :

(Save page) (Show preview) (Show changes) Cancel I Editing help (opens in new window)

Article History

Wickipedia has a facility that enables us to view the changes that have taken place during the lifespan of an article and compare past versions with the one currently on view.

• At the top of the screen, click on the tab marked **View History**.

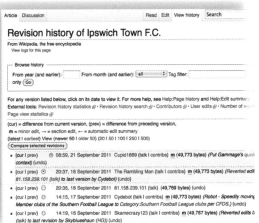

• You will find a complete history of all the changes made to this article, along with the identity of the contributors. You can compare old versions with the current one and even revert to an older version if you prefer it.

Discussing an Article

One of the most vibrant parts of Wikipedia is the **Discussion** area that every article has. Here users may argue their reasons for making alterations; in some cases this can result in so-called edit wars, where "Wikipedians" revert articles back and forth between versions.

• Click on the tab marked **Discussion**. You will see a list of all of the topics currently being discussed.

Wikispaces

http://www.wikispaces.com

California-based Wikispaces is a product of a company called Tangient. It enables users to set up their own wikis very simply and very quickly. It offers a basic free service and a more advanced subscription service for businesses. Let's look at setting a basic wiki-style webpage.

• Enter the URL: **http://www.wikispaces.com**. Complete the registration details on the front page, and click on the button marked **Join**.

• The next screen you will see is your **Welcome** page. To start your wiki, click on the button marked **Create New Wiki**. Enter the name of your Wlki and then click on the **Create** button.

• You can now begin typing text into your wiki page. If you want to add a picture, click on the **Add Image** icon (*see right*).

• In the pop-up window that follows, you can now navigate through your hard drive until you find your selected files. Click on the button marked **Open**.

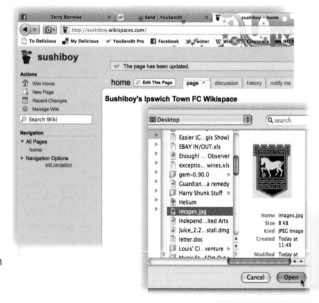

• In the **Images & Files** window, click on the **Upload** button. It's also possible to "point" to an image elsewhere on the web—to do this, type in the URL of the image and click on the **Load** button.

• Your wiki is now complete—it can now be viewed by anyone.

Wikihow

http://www.wikihow.com

Wikihow was launched with the intention of creating the world's largest how-to manual.

• To get a flavor for the information you'll find, click on **Articles**. This gives you a list of all the categories in the articles on Wikihow are listed.

• One of the most enjoyable features of Wikihow is clicking on the **Random Article** button.

Editing an Article

Now let's look at making a simple edit to an existing Wikihow article.

• On the last article we had loaded, click on the **Edit** button on the top right-hand corner of the page.

• Alter the text as required. You can see how it will look by scrolling down and clicking on the **Preview** button. If you want to retain your edit, click on the **Publish** button.

Wetpaint Central

http://www.wetpaintcentral.com

Seattle-based Wetpaint was launched in 2005 as a "wiki farm." Five years later it rebranded itself as an entertainment website for young women and hived off its wikis to a new location—Wetpaint Central. The original premise behind Wetpaint was that while wikis may be extremely easy to create and edit, they are often not very pleasant visually. One solution to this issue is to provide layout templates.

• Enter the URL: **http://www.wetpaintcentral.com**. In the main window, click on the large green button marked **Go!**

• Follow the registration and setup procedures until you are signed in. (It's slightly confusing, but Wetpaint now refers to its wikis as websites!)

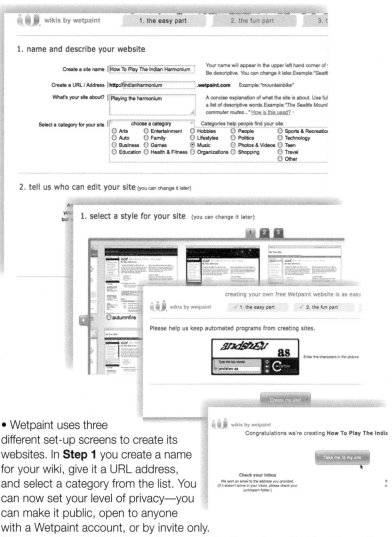

• Wetpaint uses three different set-up screens to create its websites. In **Step 1** you create a name for your wiki, give it a URL address, and select a category from the list. You can now set your level of privacy—you can make it public, open to anyone with a Wetpaint account, or by invite only. (You see, although it's being called a website, it can be edited by others, if you so choose.) When you've finished, click on the button marked **Continue to Step 2**.

• **Step 2** enables you to select a design for your wiki. If you click on one of the designs, you can see how it will appear in the **Preview** section at the bottom of the page. When you've finished, click on the button marked **Continue to Step 3**. Don't worry too much about this—you can always change it later.

• **Step 3** is a security screen. Enter the "captcha" and click on **Create My Site.** Finally, click on **Take Me to My Site**.

Adding Content to a Wetpaint Site

When you click on **Take Me to My Site**, the first thing you will see is a pop-up screen for you to send out invitations to others who might want to contribute to your page. Either complete the form and **Send Invitation** or **Cancel.**

• Begin adding content to your wiki by clicking on the **EasyEdit** button. Start writing in the main panel. You can use the commands on the **EasyEdit Toolbar** to position your text. When you are ready, click on **Save**. Your Wetpaint website is now available online.

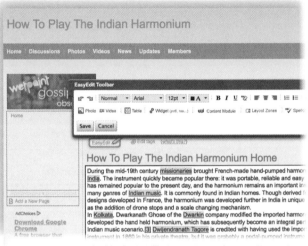

Wikibooks

http://www.wikibooks.com

Hosted by the Wikimedia foundation, built around the success of Wikipedia, Wikibooks was launched in 2003 in response to a request for a project to host and build free scientific textbooks. It works in essentially the same way as the foundation's other sites, only instead of articles these are collaborative books. Under the same umbrella, Wikijunior is a subproject for children's books.

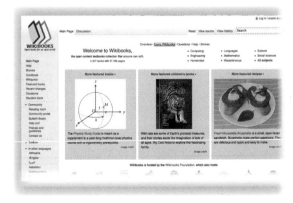

ProductWiki

http://www.productwiki.com

If you consider the powerful social networking elements of a shopping site like Amazon, where customers can review products they have bought, ProductWiki takes those aspects and wikis them up, so than any reviews can be edited by other users. It also offers where-to-buy links and ratings from other sites.

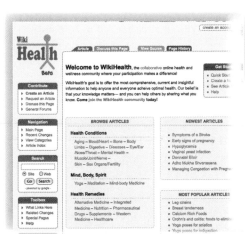

WikiHealth

http://www.wikihealth.com

A site to be approached, perhaps, with a degree of caution, WikiHealth nonetheless offers advice on a wide variety of topics, with an emphasis on "non-professional" treatments.

More Wiki Sites

Bbbuddy	http://www.bbbuddy.com	PB Wiki	http://pbwiki.com
Boltwire	http://www.boltwire.com	Qwika	http://www.qwika.com
Citeulike	http://www.citeulike.org	Reader2	http://reader2.com
Confluence	http://www.atlassian.com	Readitswapit	http://www.readitswapit.co.uk
Daisy	http://www.daisycms.org	SeedWiki	http://seedwiki.com
EditMe	http://editme.com	ShopWIki	http://www.shopwiki.com
Epictrip	http://www.epictrip.com	Sputnik	http://www.spu.tnik.org
GeniusWiki	http://www.geniuswiki.com	Tiddlywiki	http://www.tiddlywiki.com
JamWiki	http://ww.jamwiki.org	Wikihost	http://wikihost.org
LionWiki	http://www.lionwiki.0o.cz	Wikimatrix	http://www.wikimatrix.org
MediaWiki	http://www.mediawiki.org	World66	http://www.world66.com

Glossary

aggregator Software or online service that uses a web feed to retrieve syndicated web content such as weblogs and podcasts.

AJAX Abbreviation of Asynchronous JavaScript and XML, a development technology for creating interactive web applications. Works by making webpages seem more responsive by exchanging small amounts of background data with the server.

avatars Graphics used to represent people in virtual worlds. It is possible to build a character with the body, clothes, behaviors, gender, and name of your choice.

back-channel communications Private e-mails or other messages sent by the facilitator or between individuals during public conferencing.

blog An abbreviation of "weblog," a term used to describe websites that maintain an ongoing chronicle of information. A blog is a frequently updated personal website featuring diary-type commentary and links to articles or other websites. Blogs range from the personal to the political and can focus on a specific subject or a whole range of subjects.

blogroll A list of recommended sites that appears in the sidebar of a blog. These are typically either on similar topics, sites that the blogger reads regularly, or sites belonging to the blogger's friends or colleagues.

bookmarking Storing the URL address of a website either in a browser or on a social bookmarking site such as Delicious.

Boolean logic A method of combining terms using operators such as "or," "and," or "not" in a search engine.

browser Software used to view websites on computers, tablets, and smartphones. Popular examples include Microsoft Internet Explorer, Mozilla Firefox, Netscape, Opera, and Safari. Multiplatform versions exist for many of these programs.

bulletin boards Early mode of online collaboration still used in forums. Users connect with a central computer to post and read e-mail–style messages—the electronic equivalent of public notice boards.

cloud computing Term describing a shift away from the role of the desktop computer toward a remote server. Common examples include web-based software activated through a browser and remote data storage and backup.

comments Blogs and other types of applications may allow readers to add (or provide a feed for) remarks on specific items.

community building Expanding the number of people in a network by recruiting potential network participants with shared interests and goals. With more people brought into a community, the importance of the network and its usefulness to members increases.

connection The speed and nature of available Internet connection determines what tools can be used. High-speed broadband is a basic necessity for many modern web applications.

content management systems Suites of software enabling the creation of static webpages, document stores, blogs, wikis, and other tools—the Swiss Army knives of social media.

copyright The rights of the owner of a work in respect to its use.

crawler Computer robot programs (also known as "spiders" or "knowledge-bots") used by search engines to roam the Internet and catalog information.

Creative Commons A copyright license that enables an individual to allow certain controlled freedom to the sharing or reuse of their content. For example, a musician may give the end-listener the legal right to download and share a piece of music but retain the copyright with regard to its commercial distribution. Or a song may be freely sampled so long as attribution is given in any new piece of music.

default "Out-of-the-box" settings for any piece of software—can be customized to meet personal requirements.

democracy One of the buzzwords of social networking and media among those who claim the Web's potential for enabling individuals to discuss, deliberate, and take action on issues of common interest.

download To retrieve a file from a website to your computer, smart-phone, tablet, or other device.

e-mail lists Networking tools that offer the facility to "starburst" a message from a central postbox to any number of subscribers.

face-to-face (f2) Meeting people offline.

feeds The means by which you can read, view, or listen to items from blogs and other RSS-enabled sites without visiting the site, by sub-scribing and using an aggregator or newsreader. Feeds contain the content of an item and any associated tags without the design or structure of a webpage.

folksonomy A term used to describe the categorization and retrieval of webpages, photographs, links, and other items using open-ended labels called tags. Folksonomic tagging is intended to make a body of information easier to search, discover, and navigate over time.

forums Discussion areas on websites where people can post mes-sages or comment on existing messages asynchronously—indepen-dent of time or place.

friends On social networking sites, friends are contacts whose profiles have been linked to your own profile.

instant messaging (IM) Online chat with one other person using IM software such as AOL Instant Messenger, Microsoft Live Messenger, or Yahoo! Messenger. An ideal alternative to e-mails for a rapid-exchange conversation.

links Highlighted text or images that are used to navigate from one webpage or item of content to another. Bloggers make frequent use of links to reference their own or other content. Linking is another aspect of sharing, by which you offer content that may be linked and acknowledge the value of other people's contributions by linking to them.

listening in the blogosphere The art of skimming feeds to see what topics are becoming fashionable.

logging in The process of gaining access to a website that restricts access to content and requires registration.

lurkers Individuals who read forums but don't contribute. Estimates have suggested that about 1 percent of readers contribute new content to an online community, 9 percent comment—the remainder lurk.

mapping By looking at the physical connectivity of a network, mapping enables you to identify the main connecting people, and those with whom they communicate most frequently. In this way it becomes possible to evolve an online community or network from an existing "real world" network.

mash-up A new hybrid of web-based applications that mixes different services from disparate—even competing—websites. An example of a mash-up might be integrating traffic data from one source on the Internet with maps from Yahoo!, Microsoft, or Google.

membership Belonging to a group or network.

moblogging Abbreviation for "mobile blogging." Refers to posting blog updates from a cell phone or other mobile device. Mobloggers may update their websites more frequently than other bloggers, because they don't have to be at their computers in order to post.

networks Structures defined by nodes and the connections between them. In a social network the nodes are people, and the connections are the relationships that they have.

newsreader An application that gathers the news from multiple blogs or news sites via RSS and allows readers to access news from a single website or program.

open-source software (OSS) Any computer software whose source code is available under a license (or via the public domain) that permits users to study, change, and improve the software and to redistribute it in a modified (or unmodified) form. It is often developed in a public, collaborative manner.

participation Key word in social media culture used to describe the way in which people share and collaborate.

peer-to-peer (P2P) Direct interaction between two people within a network. In that network, each peer will be connected to other peers, opening the opportunity for further sharing and learning. Napster, Gnutella, and BitTorrent are examples of P2P systems.

permalink The URL address of a specific item of content, such as a blog post, rather than a website which may contain large amounts of varying content.

photosharing Uploading images to a website such as Flickr. Tags may then be added enabling others to view, comment, or even reuse those photographs.

platform The framework within which an application is able to operate. This can refer to the type of hardware used (computer, cell phone, PDA); the specific operating system (Windows, Linux, Apple Macintosh); or the nature of the application (blog, forum, or wiki).

podcast A media file distributed over the Internet, using syndication feeds, for playback on portable media players and personal computers. Although podcast content may be available as a direct download or streamed from a website, a podcast is distinguished from other digital audio formats by its ability to be downloaded automatically, using software capable of reading feed formats such as RSS or Atom.

podcaster The host or author of a podcast.

post An item on a blog or forum.

profile The information that any individual provides about him- or herself when signing up for a social networking website. This may include photographs, basic information, personal opinions, and tags that can help people searching for like-minded individuals.

proprietary software Unlike open-source software, proprietary software is owned by an organization or individual developer.

registration (*See* logging in.)

relevancy rating The most common technique for determining the order in which search results are displayed within a search engine. Each tool uses its own unique algorithm.

remixing Social media enables different content to be identified by tags, published through feeds, and combined in different ways.

RSS A family of web feed formats using the XML language and used for web syndication. RSS is used by news websites, blogs, and podcasts. RSS is widely considered to be an initialism for "Really Simple Syndication." (However, it has also been defined as "Rich Site Summary.")

search engine Information on the Internet can be found using a search engine. Along with searching by keywords or phrases, it may also be possible to search using tags that others have set up.

social bookmarking A website for sharing Internet bookmarks. Social bookmarking sites such as Delicious are a popular way to store, classify, share, and search links through the practice of folksonomy techniques. Some social bookmarking applications allow users to subscribe to feeds based on tags, thus enabling subscribers to become aware of additions on a given topic as they are created.

social media A term used to describe the tools and platforms—blogs, wikis, podcasts, photosharing websites, bookmarks, etc.—used to publish and share content online.

social software A type of software or web service that allows people to communicate and collaborate while using the application. E-mail, blogs, and even instant messaging are all examples of social software.

startpage Web service, such as Pageflakes or Netvibes, that can be configured to pull in content from a range of web-based services, such as e-mail, feeds from blogs, and news services. It is a multipurpose aggregator.

subscribing The process of adding an RSS feed to your aggregator or newsreader. This is the online equivalent of signing up for a magazine.

synchronous communications Face-to-face communication is synchronous in the same place; talking by telephone is synchronous, but in different places. The Internet extends the scope for both types of communication.

tag A keyword or term associated with a piece of information. An item will typically have more than one tag associated with it. Tags are chosen informally and personally by the author/creator, not necessarily as part of some formally defined classification scheme.

taxonomy A formal method of classifying content, such as that used in a library.

teleconferencing A meeting that takes place using a network connection without being in the same location.

threads Strands of an online conversation, whether in an e-mail or via comments on a social networking application.

tweet A message of 140 characters or less sent out via the Twitter website.

URL Universal or Uniform Resource Locator: the address on the Internet of a website or specific piece of content held on a web server.

virtual worlds Online worlds, such as Second Life, where individuals can create representations of themselves (avatars) and socialize with other residents.

voice over internet protocol (VOIP) The use of a computer or other Internet device to make and receive telephone calls. The best-known VOIP tool is Skype.

Web 2.0 A now-outdated phrase coined by O'Reilly Media in 2003 referring to a perceived second generation of web-based communities and hosted services—typically, social networking sites, wikis, and folksonomies that facilitate collaboration and sharing between users.

web-based tools Applications that function as part of a website rather than as software running on a computer.

widgets Stand-alone applications that can be embedded in other applications, such as a website or a desktop, or viewed on their own on a PDA. These may help you to do things like subscribe to a blog.

whiteboards Tools that enable users to write or sketch on a web-page. Useful in online collaborations.

wiki A collaboratively edited webpage. The best known example is Wikipedia, an encyclopedia that anyone in the world can help write or update. Wikis can be used to allow people to compose documents together or to share reference material.

Index

Acknowledgments

I'd like to thank the following people who helped out in some way with this project: John Bowers, Louis Burrows, Steve Elsey, Luke Griffin, Roland Hall, Martin Howells, Piers Murray Hill, Rachel Price, and Alex Sanders.

I'd also like to thank everyone connected with the various websites dotted throughout the book, and those who gave their assistance or permission to use their content. If any have accidentally slipped through the net please contact Carlton Books in London and they'll be put right in the next printing.

When the first edition of this book was published in 2007 I dedicated it to my then four-year-old son, Louis, who, I wrote at the time "tried his hardest to prevent me writing it at all". Four years on, and he not only helped out with checking obsolete websites, but researched and wrote the segment on kid's websites himself. So if there's a further update needed four years from now I fully expect him to handle the entire job himself. Thanks for being the greatest, B!

Terry Burrows (www.terryburrows.com)